POWERFUL
CONVERSATIONS

Credits

POWERFUL CONVERSATIONS
How High-Impact Leaders Communicate

Phil Harkins

McGraw-Hill

New York   San Francisco   Washington, D.C.   Auckland   Bogotá
Caracas   Lisbon   London   Madrid   Mexico City   Milan
Montreal   New Delhi   San Juan   Singapore   Sydney
Tokyo   Toronto

Library of Congress Cataloging-in-Publication Data

Harkins, Philip J.
    Powerful conversations: how high-impact leaders communicate / by Philip J. Harkins
      p. cm.
    ISBN 0-07-135321-6
    1. Communication in management.   2. Leadership.   3. Communication in
organizations.   I. Title.
HD30.3.H3713   1999
658.4'5—dc21   99-26326
                                                    CIP

McGraw-Hill

A Division of The **McGraw·Hill** Companies

8 9 0 DOC/DOC 0 9 8 7 6 5 4

ISBN 0-07-135321-6

The sponsoring editor for this book was Kelli Christiansen and the production supervisor
was Elizabeth J. Strange. It was set in Times New Roman by North Market Street
Graphics.

Printed and bound by R. R. Donnelley & Sons Company.

This publication is designed to provide accurate and authoritative information in regard to
the subject matter covered. It is sold with the understanding that neither the author nor the
publisher is engaged in rendering legal, accounting, or other professional service. If legal
advice or other expert assistance is required, the services of a competent professional person should be sought.

—From a Declaration of Principles jointly adopted by a Committee
of the American Bar Association and a Committee of Publishers.

McGraw-Hill books are available at special quantity discounts to use as premiums and
sales promotions, or for use in corporate training programs. For more information, please
write to the Director of Special Sales, McGraw-Hill, Professional Publishing, Two Penn
Plaza, New York, NY 10121-2298. Or contact your local bookstore.

 This book is printed on recycled, acid-free paper containing a minimum of 50%
recycled de-inked fiber

To Annette—In memoriam
Your life—Powerful Conversations that live forever

Contents

Foreword

"When Cicero spoke, men marveled.

When Caesar spoke, men marched."

HOW GREAT LEADERS achieve their status and affect change has always been of immense interest to me. When I was president at the University of Cincinnati, at the end of a busy week, I would frequently reflect on how I spent my time and what I could do to be more effective. To me, the impact and quality of leadership ultimately boiled down to one question: "Did I make a difference?" In reading this book, it occurred to me that, although a complex field of study, leadership is quite simple—it is the way great leaders communicate that sets them apart.

I thought of the above quote when I read Phil Harkins' message. While I did not necessarily intend to make men march, I wonder in retrospect how many of my own conversations could have been more powerful, and what could have been achieved as a result. Powerful Conversations—defined, analyzed, and broken down by Phil Harkins in the pages that follow—are *the* critical tool for great leaders because they lead to action and accomplishment, commitment and understanding. Like the words of Caesar, conversations that are properly aimed get things done.

These realizations played to my own experience and study of leaders. I have found, as has Phil Harkins, that great leaders speak in ways that express authenticity. They do so with a candor and clarity that allows those around them to feel their presence—to know more about not only what they want, but who they are and what they stand for. Great leaders are very clear about what they are aiming for, but they also make sure that they satisfy your agenda first. Ultimately, they achieve what they want by drawing out the greatness of those around them. They do this through the power of their conversations.

This book stands out as more than a business book. It describes how and why the best leaders connect deeply with those around them. I found it a delightful surprise, an enjoyable experience, and a journey through stories about how leaders make a difference. It was a book that made me think about the quality of every conversation I personally engage in and how I might communicate with greater power. The stories here are wonderful and sometimes even heartwarming. They will resonate with you as they have with me.

What is most impressive to me about this book, however, is that it is prescriptive. It defines in clear language the action steps you need to take to be a great communicator. Moreover, the practical tools, processes, and methods make it doable. There are parts of the book that are like a manual; I recommend you keep it close by as a reference to help you think through the important conversations you need to face. In planning meetings, speeches, and important one-on-one conversations, take the time to review the tools and action steps to ensure that your conversations are powerful. I believe that leaders who want to be "High Impact" must discipline themselves to communicate with clarity, candor, and constancy. To do so requires this level of study, self-introspection, and focus.

Leadership is hard work. Thomas Paine, in describing the tremendous endurance needed to be a soldier during the Revolution, contrasted those who stuck it out through the toughest conditions with the "fair-weather soldiers" as a great metaphor for courage. The message in this book is that High-Impact Leaders are best in adversity. Most leaders are decent enough communicators on sunny days when things are going well. The real opportunity for greatness, however, comes on those days when things are not so clear. Those are the occasions when a leader's greatness is tested, and when his or her conversations must be powerful in order to win.

It has always been wondrous to me when conversations are memorable. It is my observation that great leaders strive to make conversations lasting events. They want to be remembered for what they say and then what they do. They make sure the gray space between the two is invisible. This is because they know trust is built on commitments. They also know they will be judged not only on what they say, but what they don't say; not only what they do, but what they don't do. All of us as leaders need to think about the ways we are perceived. This book will teach you how to make a difference. It will guide you in establishing your own leadership voice in all aspects of your life.

Warren Bennis
Distinguished Professor of Business Administration
University of Southern California

Introduction

CHILDREN HAVE A WAY of getting to the heart of complex issues with a candor and clarity that adults can seldom match.

At a company party several years ago, a five-year-old approached me and asked what I did at Linkage, Inc., the company I founded over a decade ago. In trying to rise to the challenge of describing my role, I explained what the company does, what our goals are, and what we try to provide for our clients and customers. Rather than describing myself as the leader or CEO of the organization, I told him that I was like the captain of the ship—even as it occurred to me that the day-to-day running of the ship is more a matter of influence, trust, and mutual commitment than any authority or command.

He interrupted me with a certain amount of impatience and said, "No, I don't understand what you mean. Tell me what you do every day."

So, I took another tack and told him what I did in as clear a way as I could, verbally running through the events of a typical day. I mentioned meetings and telephone calls, memos, letters, and one-on-one conversations in the hallways. As he listened, I thought about how personal the interactions were and how much the success of achieving a goal depends on the state of that relationship.

He stopped me again, this time with the satisfaction of understanding, and said, "Oh, what you do is talk. That is your job."

I had to agree. When I thought about it, it suddenly seemed as clear to me as it did to him. As a leader, my role was to talk to those around me as purposefully and effectively as I could.

For the last decade, I have been studying, observing, and working with leaders in small organizations and large, across cultures and industries, from the United States to Singapore. My company, Linkage, Inc., provides organizational development programs, products, and services to Fortune 500 companies and other leading firms. For the last 30 years, I have been studying leadership. For the last 10 years, Linkage has been my laboratory.

We host major conferences that bring together the best thought leaders (like Peter Drucker, Gary Hamel, Peter Senge, and John Kotter) and CEOs (including Bob Galvin of Motorola, Max DePree of Herman Miller, and Howard Schultz of Starbucks) to discuss specific organizational and leadership development issues. Our consultants have collected data, interviewed widely, observed traits, and tested numerous theories about leadership and communication. Much of that research and field-based data provides the underpinnings for this book.

We have also pioneered action research on the competencies required for leadership, under the auspices of Linkage's Global Institute for Leadership Development, which I cochair with leadership expert Warren Bennis. Finally, I have provided ongoing consulting services for leaders at Kraft Foods, Ralston Purina, American Express, Xerox, Massachusetts General Hospital, Brigham and Women's Hospital, and many others. These executives' top priority has become the desire to communicate more effectively.

We at Linkage have developed communication tools through extensive work with leaders in their efforts to influence others, make measurable impact, and reach greater heights. Those leaders who are "best of class" we call *High-Impact Leaders,* and they use the technology of Powerful Conversations, even if they don't call it by that name.

The process of Powerful Conversations starts with an interaction between two or more people that expresses shared feelings and beliefs, progresses to an exchange of wants and needs, and closes with clear action steps and mutual commitments. Powerful Conversations advance an agenda, with all involved becoming connected to the message and the outcome. And, when action steps are lived up to, trust is fostered, bringing relationships to higher levels in preparation for the next Powerful Conversation. Powerful Conversations multiply and build a platform for smoother, quicker lines of communication. When many leaders in the same organization are engaging in Powerful Conversations, a "fast company" is the outcome.

Some people are of the opinion that working on relationships, uncovering people's wants and needs, gaining commitments, and deliberately building up trust are tasks that may result in a positive and pleasant work environment, but that are not essential to the bottom line. These people refer to such interactions as "soft stuff." They're wrong. Clear communication that moves toward results may seem easy, but it is not. In fact, communication is rarely clear, consistent, and forward moving. Rather, it usually suffers the pitfalls of misinterpreted emotion and misunderstood fact. Furthermore, most communication about difficult issues is characterized by circuitous argument, uncertain outcomes, lack of clarity, conflict in personality, and misaligned goals.

Conversations that get to underlying issues and deeply held beliefs are the "hard stuff" that can make all the difference. In the following chapters you will read about communications miscues I was called in to consult on, like the time a top executive didn't realize his boss had just fired him, or the setback of a major Wall Street firm when it lost its star $5 million analyst to a competitor because the firm wasn't listening to the analyst's needs.

The guidelines and stories that follow are based more on my personal understanding of leadership than on academic work, although there is some of that as well. I have had the privilege of working with, and getting to know, some of the best leaders from the best organizations. The meetings, speeches, and conversations of these leaders—their daily efforts at driving change and achieving objectives—are my laboratory. This book relays the lessons I have learned from these people over the years and continue to learn.

These leaders are, in fact, always doing three specific things in their conversations: (1) advancing their agendas; (2) sharing learning; and (3) strengthening relationships. It is through Powerful Conversations that they are able to obtain higher levels of trust and gain better results while creating and sustaining meaningful relationships with large numbers of their peers, bosses, and subordinates.

This book is, in essence, a handbook for those who wish to master Powerful Conversation technology so that they can develop their ability to lead and engage with those around them. It includes tools, measurements, examples, and templates you can use to deepen your knowledge and practice of this technology. Specifically, there are three sections:

- Part I focuses on defining Powerful Conversations—what they are, how they are structured, what impact they make, what objectives they accomplish, and what outputs they produce.

- Part II focuses on the practice of Powerful Conversations—how High-Impact Leaders use them in very specific ways to foster trust, drive change, retain great people, and articulate their own special voice of leadership.

- Finally, the Appendix contains a series of practical tools, such as the Leadership Assessment Instrument (LAI), that you can use to practice and master the discipline of Powerful Conversations.

The boy at the party was correct. Leaders talk. That is what they do. Leadership itself is really a series of Powerful Conversations.

Acknowledgments

THIS BOOK IS an honest journey to discover a voice of leadership. There are so many acknowledgments that go back so far that it is difficult to single out individuals who created the many ideas, various stories, and tools. I'll mention a few here. As you can see from the list, it took a huge effort from my lifetime network to create the materials contained in the book.

My special sons—Matt, Chris, and John—for the lessons you gave me on listening, letting go, and trusting, and your help in teaching me to be a good leader for you.

My siblings—Jim, Dan, Paul, Peggy, Ann, and Marie—and my mother, Anna, for caring enough and allowing me to try, and practice, Powerful Conversations with you. It is, after all, here that Powerful Conversations are most important.

My teachers, coaches, and mentors, all of you have taught me so much: Ed Keefe, CFX, Jim Lewis, vice president of Raytheon Corporation, and John Keane, Sr., president of Keane, Inc., for modeling High-Impact Leadership and showing me the possibilities; Chris Argyris, Harvard Business School and Monitor, for teaching me the fundamentals of Powerful Conversations; Fred Jacobs, American University, Paul Ylvisaker (in memoriam), Harvard Graduate School of Education, and Charlie Myers, MIT; Mike Davis, former president of Watson Wyatt (in memoriam), for giving Linkage the gift of confidence; Joe Meng, who has stood by me, providing support and counsel and demonstrating that you need not say a lot, it's more important to listen; and Warren Bennis for generously sharing his intellectual capital on leadership and unselfishly giving time.

John Kotter, Harvard Business School; Gary Hamel, London Business School; Robert Reich, Brandeis University and former Secretary of Labor;

Dan Goleman, Harvard University; Howard Schultz, Starbucks; Frances Hesselbein, Peter Drucker Foundation; Bob Galvin, Motorola; Bob Haas, Levi-Strauss; and Max DePree, Herman Miller, for the words you lent me in your speeches.

All of my clients and friends who are making Powerful Conversations a part of their life and work—thank you for your confidence and for using the tools and believing in this technology.

My colleagues and all the management team at Linkage who have been my guiding force.

The Linkage consultants who worked to develop the tools, the concepts, and the ideas, and to Linkage, Inc. for allowing these valuable tools to be displayed in this book, particularly Steve Williamson—for the theoretical framework and for designing the Tower of Power as a Linkage consultant; Jim Laughlin—for your coaching tools; LAI architects, including Rusty Sullivan, Charley Morrow, and Kerry Driscoll.

Gina Willard for all her hard work in the production of the book and Shannon Harkins and Kelly Gruber for production assistance. Kelli Christiansen, my supportive editor at McGraw-Hill, who put this on the "fast track."

The readers and critics, I remain indebted for their energy, insight, and honesty in providing feedback. Readers: Warren Bennis, Michele Bouchard, Larry Carr, Carole Cotter, Lin Coughlin, Craig Dinsell, John Doerr, David Giber, Mike Halter, Alene Korby, Todd Langton, and Ellen Wingard. Proofreaders: Martha Brown, Kerry Driscoll, Trish Griffin-Silva, Nora Hand, Tobin Kelly, Lee Langan, Suzanne Levin, Lauren O'Neil, and Michael Schultz.

Special thanks—without these great contributions from my colleagues there would be no book. Keith Hollihan—for many hundreds of hours conceptualizing, crafting, and always adding value in every way. Tireless, patient, and smart, you stood the course and made this book happen. Rusty Sullivan—only you could have made this a finished project. I am honored to work with you every day. Your humor and commitment to excellence are unsurpassed. Ellen Rosenberg—for quietly, loyally, and skillfully working to organize and pick up the pieces, never wanting the spotlight, but always deserving the honors. Caroline O'Connell—more than a publicist and an agent, you became a critically important team member contributing at all levels.

Phil Harkins
March 1999
Lexington, Massachusetts

THE DISCIPLINE OF POWERFUL CONVERSATIONS

POWERFUL CONVERSATIONS AND HIGH-IMPACT LEADERS

ALL LEADERS TALK. It is the power of their talk that determines whether they win or lose.

Think about it: the leader's most fundamental and most important job is to be in touch with those around him or her. Whether it is in the hallways or on the phone, in the middle of the workday or after hours, while delivering a performance review to a key employee or a yearly address to thousands of employees, leaders are involved in a constant series of conversations.

Through these encounters, whether brief and spontaneous or scheduled and structured, leaders try to use their time with colleagues, employees, customers, and others to reach a variety of ends. Grabbing a moment, the leader takes the opportunity to influence and direct a member of the sales staff. A weekly meeting becomes a chance to coach a manager and gather information about the department's morale and its financial numbers. A quick e-mail checks on the progress of a research project and gives a boost of recognition and support to the team. During a strategy meeting, the leader negotiates next steps with division heads and outlines a coordinated approach. At a company awards ceremony, he or she tries to hammer home a message about values and goals. In short, the leader, through his or her conversations, aims to foster relationships, build support networks, and sharpen organizational focus.

Yet outcomes from conversations are too often unclear. Perceptions don't always match. Influences are frequently not as profound as one would hope. Communication is generally a struggle with mixed, uncertain, and unpredictable results. Too much conversation is ad hoc and hinges on moods, energy levels, relationships, and personalities. Sometimes a leader is right on point. Sometimes he or she clicks and forges a new connection. Other times, the leader misses the mark. Either way, he or she pushes on, lining up the next meeting, setting up the next goal, responding to the latest need for clarification.

It doesn't have to be that way. When I first started working in industry, I recognized that there was a relationship between conversations and success. I wanted to learn more. I looked for books, manuals, or anything that could accelerate my knowledge and development as a leader, but I was frustrated because I couldn't find anything specific.

Fortunately, my answer came at my first job. It was rich with models of how to succeed through conversations. Here I watched and observed what a High-Impact Leader did and said through simple yet powerful communication. My boss, Jim Lewis, loomed above the many other leaders at Raytheon. Everyone who worked for Jim believed in his vision because he spoke from the heart. He made everything crystal clear and followed up on every promise. I immediately trusted him and knew he cared not only about me, but about all who worked for him. Everyone trusted Jim. This extended to customers, suppliers, and even competitors. He made every word impactful. It was everything that Jim said and how he said it that created his magic with people. Teams came together around Jim to do whatever it took. The lesson that I quickly learned was that there was much power in the conversations of a High-Impact Leader. I wanted to understand this so I could copy it and help others reach the same level. I realized that if Jim's conversations could create this type of unstoppable momentum, then Powerful Conversations were much more than an art form—they were a must.

Why, then, are Powerful Conversations such a burden for so many others? Is the ability to engage in Powerful Conversations a gift that Jim had, or was it a skill that he developed? It was, in retrospect, the latter.

This book is about how great leaders—deliberately, economically, and with the utmost care—maximize their conversations to achieve clear leadership goals. In fact, when it comes to great leaders, strategic and intentful communication—more than being just an afterthought—is the very key to their leadership effectiveness. I call the people who are able to do this

High-Impact Leaders, and I define their method of communication as *Powerful Conversations.*

Some dismiss the "soft stuff" of communication because it seemingly does not relate directly to results. But that is just what Powerful Conversations do: they deliver results. The leaders I know who use Powerful Conversations (whether they call their conversations by that name or not) do so because Powerful Conversations are the best, most reliable tool available for influencing others and gaining the buy-in and committed action needed to achieve real business objectives. Leaders such as Jeff Otten, president of Brigham and Women's Hospital, Mike Ruettgers, president of EMC Corporation, Steve Ozonian, president and CEO of Prudential Real Estate and Relocation Solutions, and Alene Korby, head of an operations group at Kraft Foods, would employ any tool that would help them to steer their organizations in a focused and driven way to maximize the bottom line and achieve their goals. Because Powerful Conversations deliver results, they have become one of these leaders' chosen tools.

In this chapter, I want to lay the groundwork for several concepts that are important to my theme of Powerful Conversations—and integral to an understanding of how leaders effectively drive organizational change. First, I will describe Powerful Conversations clearly and succinctly before we move on to a more elaborate picture of their complexities in the other chapters of Part I. Then, I will define High-Impact Leaders and describe who they are and what they do to make themselves so effective.

Understanding the nature of this effectiveness requires that we also introduce the importance of trust—the catalyst for turning conversations toward power. In later chapters, we will see how High-Impact Leaders, like Howard Schultz, founder and president of Starbucks, use Powerful Conversations to achieve the kinds of organizational change strategies that many of us might envision or plan, but rarely implement with the same levels of success and passionate buy-in from the major stakeholders.

THE IMPORTANCE OF QUALITY CONVERSATIONS

To recap, the basic definition of a Powerful Conversation is *an interaction between two or more people that progresses from shared feelings, beliefs, and ideas to an exchange of wants and needs to clear action steps and mutual commitments.* Specifically, a Powerful Conversation produces three outputs: an advanced agenda, shared learning, and a strengthened relationship.

How do Powerful Conversations differ from ordinary conversations? I think the qualitative differences can be intuitively understood, but let me elaborate. Clear communication that moves toward results may seem easy, but it is not. In fact, communication is rarely clear, consistent, and forward moving. Rather, it usually suffers the pitfalls of misunderstood fact and misinterpreted emotion. Furthermore, most communication about difficult issues is characterized by circuitous argument, uncertain outcomes, lack of clarity, conflicts in personality, and misaligned goals.

When good things happen and desired results come about, it is often because the participants, in the urgency of the moment, persist beyond normal bounds to knock down the barriers holding them back from committed action. When two people truly connect this deeply, there is a release, a remarkably clear understanding, and a connection that is sincere and meaningful. Both sides are clear about what needs to be done; both sides trust and understand each other that much more.

In most organizations, I have observed that this kind of conversation just doesn't happen. Wants and needs are rarely revealed, conversations skirt along at a surface level, and there is an evasion of real understanding that prevents clear, unambiguous commitments from being made. The evidence of this is that both sides at the end of a conversation frequently have vastly different understandings of what was said and what was felt—and even what was committed to and what needs to be done next. This misunderstanding can be exacerbated when both male and female leaders are involved; indeed, there is an entire body of recent research from Deborah Tannen and others concerning how gender may affect the way one receives a message. All leaders who strive to communicate more effectively need to understand and internalize how effective and impactful conversations are structured, how these conversations are entered into and resolved, and what underlying factors foster (or prohibit) deep connection and real rapport.

While the study of conversations is not new, it has nevertheless failed to receive its proper treatment as a discipline. Consider, even in light of what you have read thus far, how important conversations are to the way we function in our daily work and personal lives. Conversations are the medium through which we build relationships, make connections, develop understanding, and work and live together. Yet, as important as conversations are, it may nevertheless surprise you that we can analyze, measure, and practice them in a methodical manner. Certainly most of us never think to practice the way we interact with others. We should. Consider how much opportunity is lost because of subpar communication—and how much impact can be gained through a more willful and disciplined approach.

Recently, conversations have finally begun to receive more attention for very practical reasons. Alan M. Webber, for example, in his seminal article in the *Harvard Business Review,* "What's So New About the New Economy?", recognizes the critical role that conversations play in today's knowledge economy. Others are now recognizing that conversations are a principle driver in building that Holy Grail of our era, "the learning organization." Many researchers, including those at Palo Alto Research Center (PARC), have confirmed the necessity of the use of collaborative conversations in driving learning organizations. And conversations are finally being linked to the heart of an organization's work flow. As Juanita Brown and David Isaacs observed in their article, "Conversation as a Core Business Process":

> Consider, for a moment, that the most widespread and pervasive learning in your organization may not be happening in training rooms, conference rooms, or boardrooms, but in the cafeteria, the hallways, and the cafe across the street. Imagine that through e-mail exchanges, phone visits, and bull sessions with colleagues, people at all levels of the organization are sharing critical business knowledge, exploring underlying assumptions, and creating innovative solutions to key business issues.

Brown and Isaacs then ask us to imagine that the grapevine, which so many managers fear and discourage, is not a poisonous plant but a pathway to learning and a source of vitality.

Brown and Isaacs go further in discussing the power of conversations. They claim that these types of grapevine conversations are qualitatively different from conversations normally associated with work or sanctioned by an organization. In their research, Brown and Isaacs uncovered nine factors that made these grapevine conversations more satisfying and powerful for the participants:

1. There was a sense of mutual respect between us.
2. We took the time to really talk together and reflect about what we each thought was important.
3. We listened to each other, even if there were differences.
4. I was accepted and not judged by the others in the conversation.
5. The conversation helped strengthen our relationship.
6. We explored questions that mattered.
7. We developed shared meaning that wasn't there when we began.
8. I learned something new or important.
9. It strengthened our mutual commitment.

In essence and effect, these casual grapevine conversations establish levels of learning and trust between peers. In the same way, leaders, through the use of Powerful Conversations, are able to instill learning and trust in their colleagues and followers. It should be our objective to reach this level of connection in every important conversation we have.

Think back to a truly significant conversation you've recently had. Recall where it took place, what the circumstances were, how the conversation started, and how it ended. Then try to answer the following questions: what was it that made that conversation important? Why does it stick in your mind with a lasting feeling and bear a weight of meaningfulness? What was said during it and what was meant? What resulted from the conversation?

I am certain you will find that these three important ingredients were part of that experience:

1.   All of those involved in the conversation shared important feelings, ideas, and beliefs and made it clear to each other what those feelings/ideas/beliefs were.

2.   There were clear expressions of wants and needs that were completely accepted without judgment by all who heard them.

3.   At the end of the conversation, there was real commitment that was explicitly stated and shared with all of those who were a part of that session.

These conditions may sound more familiar to you when you think of conversations that take place in intimate or family-oriented situations. It is usually only in extremely comfortable circumstances that the barriers of fear and mistrust are low enough for the expression of true wants and needs—the conditions necessary for openness, honesty, heightened awareness, and deepened connection. How many of us have remarked or felt that we have experienced real connection, growth, and a new level in a relationship because of such a conversation?

What emerges through such connections is a deep empathy and understanding, a willingness to see other points of view, and a trustful rapport leading to clear commitment of effort and action. High-Impact Leaders are able to achieve this through the technology of Powerful Conversations. In this way, they are able to move others to accomplish great things. In a leadership team meeting recently with Prudential Real Estate and Relocation Solutions, John Van Der Wall, president of Prudential Real Estate Affiliates, observed that the essence of this technology is that Powerful Conversations spawn even more Powerful Conversations. How High-Impact Leaders create this momentum is the subject of this book.

LEARNING HOW TO ENGAGE IN POWERFUL CONVERSATIONS

When we speak of making impact through conversations, there is a tendency to take a leap and believe that in order to be a High-Impact Leader you must be a great communicator. This is a faulty premise. Being a great communicator is sometimes a gift; being a powerful conversationalist is a skill, a willful behavior learned through discipline. High-Impact Leaders understand their strengths and weaknesses in this regard, and pursue the technology of Powerful Conversations by observing the best practitioners and enlisting mentors for guidance. They do not miss any opportunities to observe how others drive teams, manage meetings, give speeches, engage in one-on-one feedback, and use language for impact.

Through this book, you will learn how to analyze your own conversational style in order to develop and use it for greater effect. As a technology, Powerful Conversations exist and can be understood on introductory, intermediate, and advanced levels. Development of any kind will have strong, positive impact on your leadership capability.

While all learning is somewhat difficult, learning as an adult can be especially hard. Relearning fundamental things such as communication can be the most difficult task of all. Many of us were raised in environments where openness and clarity were not prized. Today, we are still hardwired by that culture and upbringing. Professionally, most of us have developed as leaders within organizational cultures that are equally stifling. Even our role models in this regard no longer reflect what is required in today's world. As Aristotle suggested, the first principle of learning is accepting what you don't know. High-Impact Leaders always begin here.

If you are interested in becoming a more effective leader in your life and work, there is no more important and expedient way to achieve that goal than by absorbing and practicing the discipline of Powerful Conversations. It is my intention and hope that this book and the tools it contains will function as a manual for helping you do just that. Through an examination of Powerful Conversations, trust, and organizational change, I aim to provide a lucid understanding of what High-Impact Leaders do to make themselves so effective in achieving their personal and organizational goals.

My own journey as a practitioner of Powerful Conversations is certainly ongoing and far from complete. In the past, while leading and managing at Raytheon, Keane, Inc., and Boston University, and since founding Linkage, I have learned and relearned the power and importance of effective communication. I have found Powerful Conversations to be absolutely necessary to manage the flux of change and growth, the demands of flexible markets, and a rapidly expanding workforce. Our company, although still young, is changing and growing all the time. Without Powerful Conversations, I would feel powerless to lead it.

I am getting better at Powerful Conversations, but it is a slow, deliberate, and difficult discipline to master. Although I have researched and closely observed the ways in which great leaders use Powerful Conversations, I still struggle greatly to listen to the needs and wants of others. This is because, like many others who lead thriving organizations, I am selfish about my own needs and wants and find it difficult to think beyond my agenda. And I am like this even though I cognitively know—indeed, I am convinced through my own research—that in order to influence others and gain their trust and commitment, you must first make a connection to their wants and needs. But I am learning to live by these rules. I comfort myself with the knowledge that I have not yet met a great leader who was not acutely aware of his or her own weaknesses and constantly working on overcoming them.

High-Impact Leaders are always great learners. They purposefully try to bring their skills to the next level. They want to know more and more about how to use conversations to get done what needs to be done because they recognize that leadership is, at bottom, conversational. Leading through conversation is not an easy thing to do, and these leaders spend great time, focus, and energy honing their skills and practicing the discipline of Powerful Conversations.

THE HIGH-IMPACT LEADER
Before we go further, I want to cement a basic understanding of what characterizes and defines High-Impact Leaders.

You know them already. High-Impact Leaders are the people who get results. They are the ones who make things happen. They are the leaders who are able to continually advance a clear agenda, get others to buy into it, and move an organization, a division, or a team forward. Being a High-Impact Leader has nothing whatsoever to do with title or rank, because High-Impact Leaders can be found up, down, and across any organization.

High-Impact Leaders are the ones who cause no surprises. They are explicit, consistent, concise, and authentic. They sometimes have an abundance of charisma, but that is clearly not a prerequisite. More to the point, High-Impact Leaders are the ones who take charge wherever they are. They are the ones others *want* to follow. They are also the leaders whose teams others consistently want to join. When they move on to new roles or new territories, they do not travel alone. Others ask to go with them.

These conditions result because High-Impact Leaders use the technology of Powerful Conversations and then match what they say with what they do. Through Powerful Conversations, they develop openness, honesty, and clarity in order to get others to believe and share in their goals, to gain commitments, and to foster trust. And they prove they are worthy of that trust by delivering on their own commitments and by making results happen.

The link between Powerful Conversations and High-Impact Leaders lies in the relationship between two concepts I refer to as *Say* and *Do*. I have seen people skilled at the art of Powerful Conversations nevertheless fail as leaders because they fail to live up to their words. As a result, they never become High-Impact Leaders. I have never known a High-Impact Leader, however, who was not also skilled at Powerful Conversations, whether conscious of that designation or not. To be a High-Impact Leader, you have to be able to conduct Powerful Conversations on a consistent basis and live up to the outcomes of those conversations. Why is this important? It has to do with trust—without which conversations cannot progress toward the realization of commitments.

Let me elaborate on this point. It is only by following through on commitments and action steps that a High-Impact Leader lives up to the openness and honesty unlocked by the technique of Powerful Conversations. By consistently doing this, a leader builds trust in him- or herself and in his or her word. Failure to do so can be devastating. High-Impact Leaders are vigilant about this. They actively track and follow through on commitments because they know that leaders are judged primarily on two things: what they say and what they do.

One of the most important functions of a Powerful Conversation is to create clarity, a critical success factor for building trust. I cannot tell you how frequently I have been involved in situations in which a leader, reflecting on problems that have arisen, says, "I can't believe they thought I meant that. I never had any intention of doing that." And the followers say something like, "It's unbelievable. Our leader made a clear commitment to do this and now denies it was ever part of the agenda." Both sides shake their heads. Barriers go up. Trust is reduced or nonexistent.

True clarity implies that a leader says exactly what he or she means in such a way that his or her statements are received as intended. This requires openness, honesty, and an active and careful tracking of wants, needs, and commitments. It furthermore requires that those clear statements be lived up to with demonstrated actions.

My early family life gave me firsthand experience with the relationship between Say and Do. Clarity was not a prized value in my family, an Irish Catholic household in an immigrant neighborhood of Boston. In particular, the men in my family could not speak openly about their feelings. Leading with their vulnerabilities and clearly expressing wants and needs was completely out of the question. In this type of environment, when you don't openly say what you want and explain what you are going to do, then your partner in conversation is left with only one option: to guess at your intentions, feelings, and expectations. Such a disconnect between people causes damage beyond mere miscommunication. If you don't say very much about how you feel and what you need, those who are close to you eventually feel cheated, angry, and sometimes even hostile.

In business, the same principles apply. As a leader, do you want people to have to figure out how you feel or what you believe? Do you want your followers to have to interpret the things you don't say? Do you want people to examine your actions when they are unexplained and be forced to search for the reasons you have done something? Worse still, do you want them to feel there is no connection between what you say and what you do—that your words, the very means by which you communicate and exert your influence and power as a leader, are meaningless? What I learned in a large family environment is true to my 30 years of experience in business: such lack of clarity is dysfunctional. It creates tremendous ambiguity, which becomes the core reason many things go wrong. Organizations in which Say-Do relationships are meaningless are like modern Towers of Babel: communication is impossible and work cannot get done.

The simple diagram in Figure 1-1 illustrates the connections and disconnections between Say and Do, and how High-Impact Leaders maximize these relationships.

Leaders are obviously judged on what they say and do. Less obviously,

FIGURE 1-1   The Say/Do Matrix.

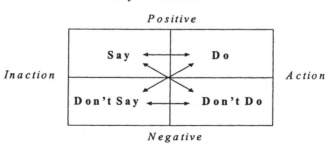

leaders arc also judged by what they don't say and don't do. What is really interesting about the matrix in Figure 1-1 is that it allows us to clearly see the importance of the diagonals, i.e., the relationships between Say and Don't Do, and Do and Don't Say. These are the areas where leaders get into trouble: when they don't do something they said they would, or when they don't say something about what they eventually do. Conversely, the best leaders do what they say, and refrain from doing what they haven't said. All of this may sound like a succession of tongue twisters. In fact, it represents the necessary bridge between having Powerful Conversations and becoming a High-Impact Leader.

THE IMPORTANCE OF TRUST

Before we embark any further on our journey of exploration of Powerful Conversations and High-Impact Leaders, we also need to lay a brief foundation on the importance of trust. I will say much more about this in Chapter 6. For now, please allow me to establish that foundation.

Gaining organizational trust has always been necessary, but it has never been more important. Within the last decade, leadership and organizational chains of command have changed drastically in our fluid knowledge economy. The old command-and-control rules no longer apply. Not so long ago, the authority and power of the head of an organization or a family was secure and unquestioned. At the most basic operating level, leader and follower were characterized by a command/perform model. The leader said "Jump!" and the follower asked, "How high?" Organizational hierarchies functioned the same way. Like the seating order at the dinner table, flowcharts clearly marked the path of decision making and command, and indicated who was to carry out directives. All in all, it was a rational means for dealing with a predictable world.

Today, though hierarchies still abound and chains of command still exist, the traditional methods for getting things done don't work quite as well as they used to. Flattened work groups, cross-functional project teams, and shifting roles have made work itself much more loosely defined and difficult to manage and organize. For the leader confronted with such conditions, the speed at which working relationships shift makes the traditional ways in which trust and understanding have been fostered—extensive face-to-face contact, a slow process of getting to know the other person—a thing of the past.

High-Impact Leaders today lead in a better way because they recognize that the shortest path to achieving objectives is to build trust and gain clear commitments from others. Specifically, they engage in Powerful Conversations to uncover the wants and needs of others in order to understand what will motivate those people to join forces with the leader and live up to the commitments of a conversation.

On a larger scale, trust is also the operating principle through which organizations foster openness and information sharing in order to make the most expeditious decisions, uncover problems, and convert ideas into action. High-Impact Leaders value trust as an asset with unlimited return. They develop the solid foundation of trust through the three outputs of a Powerful Conversation: an advanced agenda, a deepened relationship, and shared learning. Then they build upon that foundation by living up to the commitments that are the deliverables of the Powerful Conversation.

Think of trust as a bank account. Every time a leader is clear in a conversation and fulfills a commitment (i.e., makes the connection between Say and Do), he or she adds money to the account. Every time the leader fails to live up to a commitment, follow through on a conversation, or make clear the relation between his or her actions and words, the account is depleted. Too many withdrawals will result in a complete lack of trust—a condition in which no leader, however charismatic, can succeed.

So, if I make a commitment to do something in a conversation and I fail to follow through once, I may be charged only a small debit on my account. The other person might say, "Well, Phil forgot. I'm disappointed, but he's busy and has many other things to think about." If I make another commitment to that person and I don't follow through again, however, he or she will begin to suspect that my forgetfulness was willful and deliberate. He or she might think that I am ambiguous about my commitments or that what I say in a conversation is not connected with what I will do in my actions. If the pattern continues, that person will no longer trust me.

In the course of multiple interactions throughout a day, it may seem difficult or impossible for a busy leader weighted down with responsibilities to be scrupulously attentive to living up to all commitments. It is tempting for many of us to think of commitments as a nicety or a means of placating people with short-term satisfaction in the interests of fostering pleasant interactions. Such a cavalier approach comes at the expense of long-term trust.

High-Impact Leaders do not make blind requests or promises that they cannot fulfill. Instead, they skillfully orchestrate the Powerful Conversations in which they engage to make clear all parties understand the exact commitments that have been made. Then they check into those commitments and make sure through follow-up conversations that the commitments can be kept. They track the wants and needs of others and find ways to reinforce their own desire to understand the wants and needs of others, often through continued follow-up conversations. High-Impact Leaders do these things because they know that trust must exist if the leader is to achieve his or her agenda through Powerful Conversations.

ONE HIGH-IMPACT LEADER IN ACTION

I want to end this chapter with a portrait of a High-Impact Leader who effectively uses Powerful Conversations. There are any number of famous examples I could have chosen—corporate leaders, political leaders, coaches of sports teams, or leaders within the community. But I wanted to look outside these more familiar role models to highlight the fact that being a High-Impact Leader does not require a title or even an office. Let me introduce you to TJ, an outdoor adventure guide.

Last year, my three sons and I signed up with a tour group for a white-water rafting trip along 200 miles of the Colorado River. While some on the trip were experienced rafters, others, like myself, were total beginners. In order to safely and successfully negotiate the dangerous waters, 25 diverse people on two rafts had to follow the instructions of a single leader and come together as a functional team.

At 6'5" and over 300 pounds, TJ would have been impressive under any circumstances, but the power he exuded had more to do with his abilities as a High-Impact Leader than with his size. Before starting out, he gathered us around. He wore a warm smile and looked directly at each of us in turn as he explained what lay ahead on our journey and what we might expect along the path. Like a CEO warning about competition or upcoming difficulties in the next few quarters, TJ told us of the very real dangers involved with traversing over 100 rapids. At the same time, he provided us with a firm confidence in his and our own abilities, stating that he had led more than 200 journeys and had never lost anyone yet.

Though this was a paid recreational activity, a pleasure journey, it was a serious matter that required full mental preparation. I was impressed with the way TJ used strong words to establish the rules. It was with this authority and clarity that he was able to get everyone's attention and keep it.

"Taking unnecessary risks in areas above your skill level can result in serious accident or death," he said. "On any journey, falling out of the raft unexpectedly without a life jacket is very dangerous, but when passing through a level six plus rapid, it is sure suicide."

TJ asked us to pay attention to the rules in order to survive. He was also not afraid to say what he felt, or to hear in turn what we felt, when questions or concerns were raised. He made it clear what he needed from us to ensure our success and he asked openly what we needed from him to ensure our ability to succeed. Most importantly, he made clear his commitment to us and asked for our commitment in return.

I observed TJ closely during this first meeting and at other times during the seven-day journey. I could tell from the beginning that he was skilled at Powerful Conversations. He spoke without mixed messages in clear-cut terms that came straight from the heart. His eyes moved from person to person to make sure that everyone heard and understood what he was saying. He observed our body language and was quick to notice if someone was not paying attention or needed extra clarification. There was no pomp, machismo, or bragging in his tone. He openly confronted our fears about the dangers, the risks, and the elements. He was honest, clear, and committed. And we could sense all of this from the very beginning.

During the trip's seven days, we slept outside, enjoyed the breathtaking beauty of the Grand Canyon, learned about the region's history, and listened to stories and folklore. Throughout the trip, TJ spent time with each person, focusing on each of us in turn—not only to help and teach, but also to get to know us as well. He guided us along, whether we were on dangerous rapids or on water that did not have a ripple. At times, he would take calculated risks, but he always explained these clearly to us in advance. He told us what we could expect, but he also welcomed innovation along the path.

It was also interesting to see how TJ led his own staff, which accompanied us down the river, through his example and attitude. He complimented staff members when appropriate. He forgave their mistakes by acknowledging them and letting them go. He didn't allow himself to be bogged down in problems. He had no trouble in getting his staff (or us, for that matter) to work hard, because he was the one that led the way in loading and unloading the boats, cooking the food, and cleaning up. He encouraged our teams to grow in independence as time went on, even as we fully understood that he was in charge. He always displayed great enthusiasm and enjoyment and was relentlessly optimistic.

The other things I noticed were the things he didn't do. He didn't diminish the danger. He didn't say, "The boat can't turn over. Don't worry about it. Just have fun." He said, "The boat can and will turn over if we don't operate it right." But he turned fear into confidence by making indisputable statements about how safe the boats were—and reassured us that, if we acted as a team, no one would get hurt.

TJ didn't put anyone down, but he also didn't give meaningless assurances. He gave us action steps to follow and we gained confidence when following those steps translated into positive results. In this way, he created a strong team momentum, bringing together people who had never known each other before, without ever stating that as his goal. I could see, however, that he worked deliberately at maintaining relationships, both individually and with the teams collectively. We enjoyed the dividends of this—the pleasure of working together as we steered the boats down the rapids.

As a leader, TJ had a mission to guide us safely down the river. He managed to do this in a way that made it exciting and interesting. But he did more than that. He shared with us his unflagging enthusiasm and enjoyment. His ways had a calming effect and kept us going beyond what we expected of ourselves. Perhaps most importantly, he deepened our understanding and appreciation of the land we were passing through.

It was obvious to me that he had a purpose and strategies and tools for reaching his goals. Even though he plainly had never heard of the term *Powerful Conversations,* he was using them to promote learning, deepen relationships, and advance an agenda. He knew what he was doing and what he needed to do. He knew, in essence, his own leadership profile—his strengths and weaknesses as a leader.

At the end of the trip, I spoke privately with him. I told him that I had been observing his leadership abilities throughout the week. He laughed and asked me what I had seen.

I told him about his leadership profile and about what I saw as his strengths and competencies. I also told him about the areas where I thought he was probably working the hardest to compensate for his weaknesses. He told me I was exactly right. He had been working to develop these areas all his life. He asked me what he could do to be a better leader.

I shouldn't have been surprised, even then at the edge of the Colorado River. It fit completely with my experience of High-Impact Leaders, no matter the setting: they are always pushing themselves and striving to know more in order to improve.

High-Impact Leaders constantly look for ways to grow and become more impactful. It is my hope that, by introducing you to the tools and applications of Powerful Conversations, this book will help you to become a more impactful leader as well.

2

THE STRUCTURE AND IMPACT OF POWERFUL CONVERSATIONS

WHEN MOST OF US communicate, goals and desired outcomes are hit or miss. We might get lucky in advancing our agendas; we infrequently consider learning as a critical outcome; and we hope not to damage the relationship too badly along the way. So in talking with another person in the course of a busy day, we dust off the relationship, share a laugh or a complaint, and, for the most part, only incrementally improve our ability to connect. More likely than not, we simply maintain the status quo, put a few patches on the leaks in our information, and move on.

With High-Impact Leaders, it's different. They see their conversations not as a challenge or a means for survival, but as an opportunity. Specifically, they achieve their goals by clarifying commitments and creating next steps—and they do so in ways that promote learning and measurably improve relationships. In this chapter, I want to focus on how High-Impact Leaders accomplish all of this by consciously paying heed to the building blocks of Powerful Conversations.

In case any doubt remains, please allow me to dispel it now: this book is not about the soft stuff. Powerful Conversations are a concrete tool used by hard-hitting leaders at organizations such as Kraft Foods, Baystate Health System, Xerox, Prudential Real Estate and Relocation Solutions, and Ralston Purina, to name just a few. High-Impact Leaders in these companies engage in Powerful Conversations consciously, deliberately, and systematically. High-Impact Leaders in numerous other organizations I have observed use Powerful Conversations in an implicit fashion: they may not refer to "Powerful Conversations," but they practice the discipline and adhere to its principles nonetheless. They, too, intrinsically know that communication is actually the hard stuff—and the stuff that delivers results.

THE COSTS OF STATUS QUO COMMUNICATION

In most organizations today, too much time and energy are wasted on communication. The waste lies not in the effort but the effectiveness. Leaders in these companies try to communicate effectively, but they largely don't succeed. The net result: less efficiency, effectiveness, and productivity, and more missed opportunities that would have been capitalized upon if people were communicating powerfully. I would take this a step further: I believe that organizations rise or fall based on the power of the conversations taking place within them.

Powerful Conversations are, among other things, a way to drive out the dysfunctionalities within your organization. They are also the key to unleashing the real power inside individuals within your organization. Powerful Conversations breed a powerful organization. Ineffective communication, on the other hand, results in a trail of lost opportunity.

Consider, as an example, the high-tech wars of the 1980s. As a vice president at Keane, Inc.—then a blossoming start-up, now a billion-dollar company—I was a witness to (and sometimes a participant in) these wars. Time and again, I saw companies underperform when their leaders were not talking and listening effectively. This reinforced for me how collaborative communication, openness, and trust fundamentally improve an organization's ability to compete, grow, and respond to rapid change.

Twenty years ago, Digital Equipment Corporation (DEC) led the way with small and mid-range computers. (Microsoft and the other industry titans today were not even on the radar screen.) DEC stands out not only because of its early success, but because of its dramatic fall. When new markets emerged in personal computers, software, and systems integration, DEC stuck to its traditional business despite the warnings of its smartest people and its best customers. DEC's leaders (Ken Olsen and his top lieutenants) were so grateful to the technology that had gotten the company so far so fast that they didn't want to hear what others were saying, both within and outside the organization, about the imminent obsolescence of that technology. People told DEC's leadership that the company had to switch gears, but they soon realized that their warnings were falling on deaf ears. Eventually, they stopped telling.

Many of DEC's best people left in frustration. Some of these people ended up leading the organizations that would eventually overwhelm DEC when the industry indeed turned. DEC's failure to keep pace wasn't due to the fact that it lacked the resources to compete in these new markets, for DEC had capital like no other company in the industry. The problem was all about communication—the good ideas simply weren't getting out into the open and weren't being heard. By 1998, DEC's fall was complete: it had lost so much market share that Compaq was able to snatch it up.

Even at Keane, a great success by any standards, I look back and know the company could have done even better in creating a forum for new thinking and ideas. For example, I remember talking to a young man who worked for me named Eric Bedell. He was passionately excited about a dramatic new idea he'd heard the night before at a Boston Computer Society meeting. A fellow named Mitch Kapor had spoken to the group about his vision of applying PC technology to spreadsheets. It may sound like common sense today, but it was a radical idea for the time. That night, Kapor also made what amounted to an open plea for help in building his new company. Eric was interested in the idea—for Keane. We had an open culture, but not one that would seriously entertain such a radical idea. I tried in vain to dissuade Eric with strong warnings about the weaknesses of this new small-market computing, but he felt strongly about the market's potential. So he left Keane and went to work for this start-up, a company called Lotus Development Corporation. The next time I saw Eric, he was in a limo at Kennedy Airport and I was waiting for a taxi in the rain.

All organizations make mistakes. The best organizations constantly work to identify and rectify the communication failures and gaps that underlie those mistakes so that the same mistakes won't happen again. Hewlett-Packard, the only hardware manufacturer of any size and scope that has stayed near the top as the DECs of the world fell, leads by a principle of collaborative interaction. The leaders there encourage people to dig down into what they are really thinking to unearth the best ideas and discover the real opportunities. This is the same principle behind Microsoft's famous "e-mails to and from Bill." It's also how Cisco Systems operates, motivating people in the organization to speak up and express what's really going on. High-Impact Leaders use the most effective ways available to communicate with people because they know they cannot possibly see what is around the next corner. And you can never predict who within your organization will stumble onto the next big idea. That is why every conversation is critical.

That is also why High-Impact Leaders prepare for their conversations—so that they can make the most of their interactions. Mike Ruettgers, president of EMC Corporation, carries a notebook with him wherever he goes. In that notebook, he painstakingly records what people tell him and what he tells people. He doesn't want to lose track of an idea. Nor does he want to break a commitment he makes. Mike Ruettgers did not start off being a naturally gifted communicator, but he worked at it. He did this through deliberate and structured usage of Powerful Conversations technology. Today, it is one of the most effective tools in his leadership arsenal for driving conversations toward results. If Powerful Conversations weren't about results, then Mike Ruettgers wouldn't bother. But they do lead to results. So Mike Ruettgers uses them.

The ability to generate and manage quality conversations distinguishes effective leaders. It is the way they share critical business knowledge, ask tough questions, test assumptions, and catalyze action. It is the means through which they initiate requests and obtain commitments. It is how they get results. And natural-born communication skills have nothing to do with it.

THE STAGES OF A POWERFUL CONVERSATION

All leaders who strive to communicate in more effective ways need a clear understanding of how Powerful Conversations are structured and how they forge a deep connection between participants. To that end, let's examine the progression of a Powerful Conversation.

A Powerful Conversation typically proceeds in three stages.

- *Stage One.* In the beginning of a Powerful Conversation, the initiator of the conversation sets up his or her agenda with an honest feeling or a sincere expression of need. For our purposes, I use the term *agenda* to describe a desired outcome—that is, a goal or a set of goals that require the cooperation, support, and commitment of one or more persons. The statement of an honest feeling or a sincere need signals to the other participant(s) in the conversation the importance of the agenda. It also constitutes a request for help and contribution.
- *Stage Two.* In the middle of a Powerful Conversation, there is a discussion of the issues enmeshed in the agenda. A High-Impact Leader skillfully probes for the wants and needs of the other participant. In

this way, he or she uncovers the goals of the other person(s) that must be met in the process of achieving the leader's own agenda. This is the stage where the High-Impact Leader surfaces any hidden agendas and connects facts with underlying assumptions in order to advance his or her agenda.

- *Stage Three.* In the closing stage of a Powerful Conversation, the High-Impact Leader makes sure the participants have nailed down the next steps and are open about what they will do to make those commitments come to life. The closing of a Powerful Conversation is also the time when a High-Impact Leader asks openly whether the other person really got what he or she wanted in that conversation. This is a good way to ensure that a Powerful Conversation will lead to results.

Stages aside, you can always tell whether you have had a Powerful Conversation by examining the conversation for three outcomes:

1. Advancement of an agenda
2. Shared learning
3. A stronger relationship

I call these the three measurements of a Powerful Conversation. They are the telltale signs that reveal whether a Powerful Conversation has taken place. When it indeed has, there is a furthering of trust—and a feeling that next time the parties will reach agreement and advancement of mutual agendas that much faster.

THE BARRIERS TO REAL CONNECTION

It is essential not to skip a stage when progressing through a Powerful Conversation. Otherwise, you can fall into the trap of leaping forward in an undisciplined way. The commitments that result from such conversations are frequently shaky.

It is the initial stage of the Powerful Conversation—the honest feeling, the sincere expression of need—that presents the most challenges for a High-Impact Leader. This isn't because High-Impact Leaders are less humane or emotionally attuned than others. Rather, the difficulty lies in the fact that High-Impact Leaders are typically driven, focused, and optimistic of outcome. They therefore find it hard to take the time to make a real connection and express any fear, worry, or need.

A leader, by most accepted understandings, has a healthy ego, is a model of confidence, and stands as a paragon of strength. Showing weakness or emotion is considered a mistake. In fact, however, exhibiting honest vulnerability is the key to making connections with other people—the initial opening that allows a Powerful Conversation to take place and gives the leader the license to lead.

As Howard Schultz, CEO of Starbucks, said in an interview with Linkage's Global Institute for Leadership Development in 1997:

> I think every leader has to be honest. I did an interview at NPR last week and the person asked me, 'What's the most important quality today for leadership?' I said to him, 'I'm going to give you a surprising word and you're going to be taken back by it.' It wasn't something I thought about, just something that came to me, and that is to display *vulnerability*.

The use of Powerful Conversations technology requires us to be open and honest about our feelings, including our needs and weaknesses—or, as Schultz says, our vulnerabilities. For many leaders, relentlessly driven, focused on their own agendas, obsessed with bottom-line results, this is the reason Powerful Conversations are so difficult to practice in the first instance.

What Howard Schultz says about vulnerability is true. Vulnerability allows us to open up the wants and needs of others. As Schultz went on to express in the same interview:

> Sometimes we don't have all the answers, sometimes we make mistakes . . . It's really a question of being honest and open, sharing the vulnerabilities and sometimes the insecurities. And I think people today want their leaders to display the balance of the human condition. I also think these are gradual steps that people are going to need to take. People are going to need to build bridges and look for small victories. But the people that I'm around—and it's really my peer group which is young or relatively younger CEOs—represent a different kind of leader and a different kind of manager today.

When it comes to emotion, however, too many leaders are risk averse. There is nothing more difficult to acknowledge than embarrassment, emotion, weakness, and anxiety—not to mention simple wants and needs. It is only through honesty about our emotions and needs that we are able to really connect. It was five years ago, on a very sad day, that I first truly learned this lesson. I was taught by a person who practiced Powerful Conversations every day of her life that I knew her.

I include this story in all humility as an ode to someone whose wisdom about communication goes far beyond where I have gotten, despite my best efforts. The story is not intended to make you feel melancholy about another person's sadness and I do not include it in a business book lightly. It is a story that vividly illustrates the way fear of emotion serves as a barrier to connection, and I have included it only for that purpose.

The horrible news arrived on the first day of Lent, on an otherwise bright, springlike day in Boston. The diagnosis was conclusive. Annette, my wife, had a severe type of leukemia. They called it acute miloblastic, which simply meant that the leukemia was fast moving and spreading like crazy among the trillions of cells in her body. There was a slim hope: 20 percent of cases in recent years had been treated to the point where they were under control and in remission. But we faced an imminent and profound change that neither of us had ever really expected. The treatment plan was to be excruciating, with no great promise of recovery. It was to begin immediately—the next morning, in fact—canceling our first vacation together in five years.

Inside, my emotions were overwhelming. I was apprehensive, gloomy, dismal, and devastated. If I had to define only one feeling, I could do no better than to recall a deep and frantic worry about everything. Not wanting to address fear or acknowledge my worry, I gave my best, most optimistic pitch in the car on the way home. My talk continued as we pulled into the driveway and even as we settled into our living room. I told my wife how we were going to beat the odds. In fact, I insisted that the odds were in our favor, given Annette's strength and her other special qualities.

It seemed the right thing to do. Rather than deal with the worry and the fear, or the things I needed, or more importantly, the things that Annette needed or the commitments we would need to make to go through this together, I continued to spew positive messages to a woman who listened patiently until I finished.

When I sat down next to her, she grabbed my hand and said words that I will never forget. She said, "I really need to talk with you about how I feel and I need to know more about how you feel because I know you are worried. I need to talk with you about what I want and what I need. Because there is so much to say and so little time now to talk about this. Would you make a commitment to put away your optimism for a moment and tell me what is going on with you?"

As she held my hand and looked in my eyes, I knew that all my "powerful" words of optimism were not powerful at all. They didn't disguise anything about my feelings. They didn't diminish the worry. They didn't change reality. With her words, I fell apart. But we were then able to have a Powerful Conversation, the most powerful of our lives together. I listened to her explain her feelings. She told me of her fear and worry. It was not about dying or the pain, but about knowing that everyone else would be okay.

We faced up to the real wants and needs regarding the treatment plan. We made commitments that we both lived by throughout the most awful period of physical pain one could imagine. During that very long year of illness, we had other Powerful Conversations (although we didn't refer to them as such). I felt and understood that the conversations were powerful because we continued to communicate our needs and meet our goals together. We both grew enormously in spiritual ways, as well as through a deeper learning about each other and about life. Day by day, our relationship became even stronger.

The lessons I have learned in business pale to what I learned through that journey. But it was clear to me later how universal the issues of communication are—indeed, that a conversation that advances trust in a business relationship is only removed from such deeply personal connections by a matter of degree rather than of kind. I also learned that it is possible to face the most important things in life this way. I remind myself of that when I deal with difficulties related to business or other aspects of my personal life.

I can see parallels in my career with how I acted in first talking with Annette. Rather than dealing directly with difficult emotions and uncertain situations, I typically prefer to avoid them. My first and strongest instinct is to use optimism to skirt around fears or concerns. I know now that I should be clearly expressing my worries and confronting what is actually going on in order to find real solutions, yet I still often stumble on exactly the same hurdle. You would think I had learned a lesson overwhelming enough not to have such difficulties repeat themselves, but I continue to need to relearn. I find as well that this is the hardest part in training other leaders in the practice of Powerful Conversations. I comfort myself with the observation that others frequently exhibit this same tendency. It must be something basic to being human.

ORGANIZATIONAL DEFENSES AND UNDISCUSSABLES

Most of us in the workforce find little reason to open up. Guardedness, half-truths, hidden dialogue, and other "organizational defensive routines," as Chris Argyris, my former professor at Harvard, calls them, are the normal way of doing business. Opening up obviously does not always entail expressions of strong feelings and caring such as in the story I just relayed, but it is critical nonetheless. In business and in life, the difficulty of being open can (and probably more frequently does) refer to the emotional content around facts and hard truths.

There is nothing harder than honesty about real work and organizational issues. Sitting down with the CFO if you are a project head, or standing before the global sales force if you are a CEO, will bring out a range of conflicting impulses. Many of us readily, naturally, and willingly mix truth with half-truth, optimistic visions with achievable realities.

Chris Argyris described this phenomenon well in 1990 in his book, *Overcoming Organizational Defenses:*

> Whenever human beings are faced with any issue that contains signifi- cant embarrassment or threat, they act in ways that bypass, as best as they can, the embarrassment or threat. In order for the bypass to work, it must be covered up. The basic strategy involves bypass and cover up.
>
> Because most individuals use these actions, the actions become part of the fabric of everyday life. And because so many individuals use these actions frequently, the actions become organizational norms. The actions come to be viewed as rational, sensible and realistic.

It happens between individuals and it happens organization wide. Argyris, crediting author Peter Block for pushing forward our understand- ing on this issue, then notes that the logic of organizational defensive rou- tines is based on four premises:

> (1) craft messages that contain inconsistencies, (2) act as if the messages are not inconsistent, (3) make the ambiguity and inconsistency in the message undiscussable, and (4) make the undiscussability of the undis- cussable also undiscussable.

All of this happens between individuals and on a more organization- wide basis. It happens in big situations and small. Organizational defensive routines are why the Challenger disaster occurred and how Ken Olsen & Co. lost the rudder at DEC. It's the dance a parent and child go through dis- cussing homework and grades. It's what takes place under the surface in the performance review meeting that doesn't get at the painful truths necessary for both parties to push forward and grow.

When I think of the "undiscussable," I think of the behavior I observed at a meeting of the senior leadership group of a large, professional services company with 80 offices worldwide.

Prior to the meeting, I had discussions with two of the seven members of the group. Both told me that they believed that the sales compensation system was negatively impacting sales and had to be changed. They spoke openly about how the organization was moving in the wrong direction as a result of the incentives used with the sales force. They expressed these feel- ings clearly—passionate in their belief that this had to be changed for the organization to reach its agreed-to growth objectives.

The president of the organization was known to have different feelings about the current incentive program. As the original architect of the plan, he had championed the framework and held onto it throughout the years.

The meeting was specifically set up to look at the possibilities of correcting the sales efforts, which had begun falling short as of late. A number of ideas came up at the meeting on how to increase the number of targeted accounts and the penetration of accounts. The team also discussed realigning sales territories, hiring more sales associates, leveraging the senior leadership on sales calls, and conducting marketing and direct mail campaigns. But no one brought up the sales incentive program the two senior leaders had complained about to me prior to the meeting.

At the end of the meeting, all of the senior leaders rank-ordered the list of tactics and did normative group voting to define three modes of attack. As the meeting ended, they laughed and encouraged each other, spent a few minutes socializing in a relaxed atmosphere (with hands in pockets and much laughter), and casually mentioned other concerns and upcoming plans. I could not help but wonder what they really felt they had accomplished, and whether they really believed that this meeting had been effective or powerful. Indeed, would the commitments made within the meeting really result in the bottom-line improvements they were looking for?

I later called both leaders who had mentioned to me their private concerns about the sales incentive program and asked them how they felt the meeting had gone. Their attitudes were similarly positive. I referenced their earlier comments. Neither seemed upset that the program had gone undiscussed. One of them said, "I decided not to go there. I've been there before and it just wasn't the right time to discuss it."

I pressed him. I wanted to determine how he had really perceived the meeting's results, given that the incentive program had gone unaddressed. "Didn't you tell me it was the only way to get the numbers? You kept talking about the need for major surgery." He made his case for the quality of the meeting. "Yes," he said, "you're right. But maybe we can do enough to get close by taking on the approaches that came up in the meeting."

I was amazed at the gap between his old convictions and his new attitude, so I continued to dig. We backed up and talked about his feelings about day-to-day operations, and eventually the topic of the meeting came up again. This time, he was more honest. He told me he didn't feel that they had advanced toward any kind of important goal. There hadn't been any mutual learning. It was a meeting like any other meeting, ending in a list and a good feeling. There was an unspoken sense that any real work would take place later, in the trenches—if at all.

The meeting had maintained relationships and placated the president. But it didn't examine anything hard. Nothing powerful emerged, not even in the maintaining of those relationships. None of the participants felt that they had uncovered something important or learned something new. None believed they were actually going to accomplish something significant. In a sense, the meeting was a social ritual that had little to do with its stated goals.

This gap between reality and perception is at the root of what organizational psychologists are examining when they refer to *mental models*. Mental models are interrelated sets of ideas, beliefs, values, and assumptions about how the world works (and should work). They are important to understand because they underlie our commitments, focus our emotional energy, and influence our ability to deliver on what we vocalize.

The senior leader's perceptions of the quality of the meeting indicated a misalignment between his mental model and what had actually happened: he truly believed that the group needed to address the sales incentive program (his mental model), but the group addressed other side issues instead. Powerful Conversations, through their rigor and structure, demand that we get to the inner sanctums of the hidden dialogue between people. They unearth the "undiscussables" that people, in fact, want to discuss. Power is unleashed when people are able to talk about their real thoughts, feelings, assumptions, and needs in a focused and results-oriented way.

CLOSING THE DOOR TO OPEN UP

What happens when the undiscussables never get discussed? Consider the following story. Two years ago, I was consulting to a Wall Street equity analyst about his firm's recent turnover problems. The firm had just lost three of its top analysts to a rival investment bank. I had been asked to talk with this analyst in order to understand what had happened. Getting to the real facts behind the situation proved, not surprisingly, to be a challenge.

This senior analyst was a great success on Wall Street, just as he had been in a prior career with a major industrial giant. Our conversation, however, began in a relatively bland fashion. I asked what the analyst thought was driving the departures of key staff and listened politely and quietly to his answers. He cited the usual litany of problems with the firm, deficiencies in the senior leadership, and so on.

When he took a breath between sentences, I began to probe deeper. I asked him how he felt about what had happened—how it impacted him and what he needed and wanted. I asked him what he required from the organization in the way of help. I inquired about the kinds of commitments he would need theoretically to be kept inside of the organization.

He interrupted with a strong look. Instead of beginning to speak he stood up, walked over to the door, and closed it. Then he returned and sat down.

"Do you want to know how I really feel?" he asked. Knowing he did not require an answer, I only nodded. It was from this point that we really connected. He told me what he really felt and what he believed the organization needed. In other words, he discussed the undiscussables.

It was the act of closing the door that I found myself thinking about later. It was as if he could only open himself up by closing access to himself in other ways. What was it that released the analyst from his guardedness? By merely closing the door and shutting off the organization at large, he became more open. It was a fascinating gesture, one you may also have observed in organizations as a necessary condition (and symbolic kickoff) for an honest conversation.

What prompted the analyst to get up and close the door was the nature of my questions. I demonstrated sincerely that I wanted to know what was going on from his perspective. Recognizing the honesty of my inquiry, he was moved to reveal his own hidden dialogue. And he felt that hidden dialogue could only be revealed in a hidden place. How much better would that firm have been if openness prevailed—if people felt free to reveal their true wants and needs without having to close their doors? If such an atmosphere had been present, I assure you I wouldn't have been privy to it: the three top analysts wouldn't have left and I wouldn't have been called in to help deal with the situation after the damage had already occurred.

THE IMPORTANCE OF LISTENING

It is by demonstrating sincere interest in another person's real thoughts and feelings that a leader is able to tap into hidden dialogue, surface the undiscussables, and uncover wants and needs. By being a skilled listener, a High-Impact Leader can sort out the content of this hidden dialogue into important facts and assumptions.

There are four important principles involved in becoming a great listener:

1.   Focusing in a visible way
2.   Sorting and compartmentalizing needs and wants
3.   Recognizing the feeling as well as the content
4.   Balancing inquiry, advocacy, and judgment

Being able to listen intently to another person is a great gift. It is critical that you visibly focus, without distraction, on the words another person is speaking along with the feelings he or she is relaying. There are two components here: you must actually be listening, and you must visibly be showing that you are doing so. Only then will the speaker feel compelled to speak in total candor. Active listening, then, helps lower the barriers blocking a Powerful Conversation.

Many political leaders have mastered this art. They exude a sense of intimacy that creates a feeling, in return, that the person listening is worth following. John F. Kennedy was one such politician. In an interview with Arthur Schlesinger, Jr., Isaiah Berlin explained why Kennedy was such a great listener:

> He listened with extreme intentness. This was one of the things which struck me most forcibly. I've never known a man who listened to every single word that one uttered more attentively. His eyes protruded slightly, he leant forward toward one, and one was made to feel nervous and responsible by the fact that obviously every word registered. And he replied always very relevantly. He didn't obviously have ideas in his own mind which he wanted to expound, or for which he simply used one's own talk as an occasion, as a sort of launching pad. He really listened to what one said and answered *that*.

Great listeners also demonstrate the ability to sort out what is really being said in a conversation. Through close listening, they can separate what a person wants (a "nice-to-have") from what a person needs (a "have-to-have"). Then, too, most communication is filled with indirect expressions, as well as nonverbal language. Body language usually comprises a big part of the message. The average person focuses intently on the content of the message and totally misses the feeling behind the content. High-Impact Leaders recognize such feeling and make it a point to let others know they have grasped the feeling in addition to the words.

The other principal skill of great listeners is that they are able to balance inquiry, advocacy, and judgment. They inquire in a nonjudgmental way, so that they can understand the facts behind the facts. At the same time, they project that they are on your side and will advocate on your behalf. And, at the end of the day, they possess the judgment necessary for proper interpretation. Again, John Kennedy serves as an example. In the words of Isaiah Berlin:

> [T]he point about him was that he gave one the air of luminous intelligence and extreme rationality, and cutting through a lot of dead wood. He

didn't accept loose or vague statements, or the kind of general statements which people make who haven't very much to say but feel they ought to make some contribution to the conversation, simply as a form of registering the fact that they are present and have views.

Whenever that kind of statement was made by any of us, he stopped us short and asked us exactly what these words meant, and brought it all down to extremely clear and shining brass tacks.

Kennedy's inquiry, along with his advocacy and judgment, go a long way in explaining why he was such an effective and impactful leader. He didn't listen simply to show that he cared, or because he was interested in scoring points with the other person. He listened, like all great listeners, because he was intensely interested in the information. He knew that the best way to uncover facts was to connect in a deep and intimate way.

THE TOWER OF POWER

Most of us are not natural communicators like John Kennedy. For those leaders who lack that innate ability but nevertheless wish to make deep connections, listen intently, uncover hidden dialogue, and progress toward mutual commitments and action steps, the Tower of Power is a tool well worth understanding and using.

The Tower of Power (see Figure 2-1) is a four-step plan that allows a conversation to move through the three stages of a Powerful Conversation discussed earlier—from an expression of honest feelings (Stage One), to an

FIGURE 2-1   The tower of power.

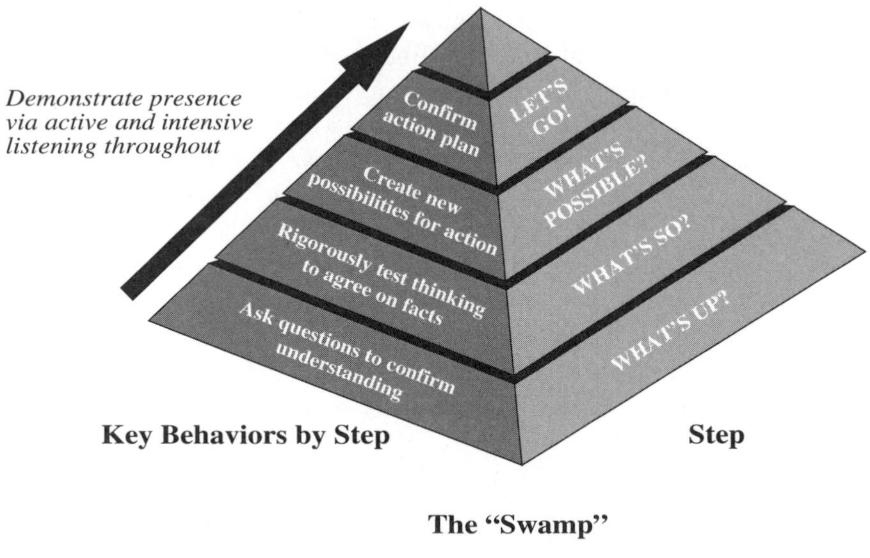

The "Swamp"

examination of mutual wants and needs incorporated in an agenda (Stage Two), to, finally, an establishment and confirmation of clear commitments that will lead to action (Stage Three). The Tower is also a tool for ensuring Powerful Conversations. If you conduct your conversation by faithfully and successfully working your way up the Tower, you will have had a Powerful Conversation. It is, in fact, impossible to have a Tower of Power conversation that does not result in advanced agendas, shared learning, and strengthened relationships—the very measurements of a Powerful Conversation.

Many High-Impact Leaders internalize the steps of the Tower in order to prod and guide the conversation toward desired results. Alternatively, others openly use the Tower as a framework with their conversation partners so that they can proceed together toward Powerful Conversations. In an operations group at Kraft Foods, for example, diagrams of the Tower of Power are on the walls of meeting rooms and offices. They are there to remind people how conversations should progress in the name of effective and impactful communication. As Kraft has proven, you can bring the Tower out in the open. It is not a tool a leader needs to hide like a magic card.

Here are the four steps involved in using the Tower of Power to structure your Powerful Conversations.

Step One: "What's Up?"
In this initial step, a High-Impact Leader strives to make emotional connections with the other person so that that person, in turn, will open up, share hidden dialogue, and reveal undiscussables. The High-Impact Leader is trying simultaneously to express his or her own agenda, wants, and needs, and to uncover the agenda, wants, and needs of the other person. High-Impact Leaders know that in order to advance their own agendas, they must also advance the agendas of others. They know that in order to fulfill their own wants and needs, they must likewise fulfill the wants and needs of others.

This knowledge is based upon the difference between pushing and pulling in a conversation. People who have studied the power of language are aware of the connection between uncovering strong feelings and expressing undiscussables. Researchers such as Fernando Flores advocate speaking with intention because actions result from words. A January 1999 *Fast Company* article describes a workout session between Flores and a team of senior leaders needing a transformed language for effective communication. In the article, Flores states that trust and openness require truth. But he seeks truth through abrupt, almost abusive confrontations in which honesty is purposely hostile. For example, he instructs partners in conversations to state negative opinions first. Under his methodology,

Flores heaps scorn on executives until their anger and frustration boil over, eventually creating a new, relaxed, and open mood. While the technique may work in the short term and under the lab-like conditions of a closed session, such a "pushing" approach does not yield long-term connection, genuine honesty, and real trust.

More effective and lasting connection comes through pulling, not pushing. It is why leading with vulnerability is so necessary. It draws others in, rather than forcing them to comply. It is why a High-Impact Leader will open a conversation with a statement like, "I need to talk about this situation because I am concerned about us reaching our goals," rather than an admonition like, "We have to talk about your poor performance in order to rectify what you are doing wrong."

Step Two: "What's So?"
In this step, the focus is on determining the hidden factors underlying the issue or problem.

Typically in conversations, people are used to moving rapidly from facts to inferences and assertions. Building on Chris Argyris's work, Peter Senge has described this kind of learning and discovery as *adaptive,* because it involves doing the same thing in patterned ways, over and over again, with minor adaptations. Leaders need to do more. They need to probe and question in order to establish fact and the soundness of the reasoning that lies behind assertions. Rigorous thinking is required. If emotional connection is soundly established in the "What's Up?" step, both parties can join with equal enthusiasm and effort (and with little fear and defensiveness) in uncovering the real assumptions and facts underlying an issue. Senge calls this kind of learning *generative* because it takes understanding to the next level, resulting in new designs and new ways of looking at things. There is no way to get to generative learning unless undiscussables are surfaced.

Think back to the example cited earlier of the seven leaders gathered to discuss how to increase sales and hit growth objectives. Suppose the atmosphere in that room had been devoid of organizational defensive routines. The president might then have been able to say:

> I feel we have to look again at the fundamental systemic issues that are adversely impacting our ability to be able to sell and reach our growth objectives. I want to be sure we examine all of our assumptions governing our thinking and ask each other hard questions, openly and honestly. I would like you to know that I will put away all of my prior assumptions and listen closely. This is my commitment in starting this meeting because

I need and want us to get where we have to be. It is my fear that some of our prior discussion on this has choked off thinking and may have led us to error.

The results of such a meeting would have been drastically different from what actually happened, both in feeling and outcome.

Step Three: "What's Possible?"
This is the step of the Tower of Power that is too frequently skipped. Once participants have uncovered the assumptions and facts during the "What's So?" step, they are eager to jump directly into an action plan. It is important, however, to take extra time to imagine alternatives and forge creative solutions that might result in smarter business decisions beyond the obvious. To reiterate: don't omit the "What's Possible?" step.

A High-Impact Leader challenges the people on the other side of the conversation to stretch their thinking and go beyond the boundaries of what they believe to be possible and most appropriate. In the best conversations, the "leader" and "follower" build off one another's ideas to create new insights and possibilities. This is where great partnerships or great teams work so well. Enjoying the interplay and synergy of each other's logic and unique perspective, remarkable in their rapport, the participants leap toward possibilities with shared intuition. Those who have experienced this in its highest form are aware of its rare and significant value.

Step Four: "Let's Go!"
The final step of the Tower of Power involves making a confirmed and mutually understood commitment to action. It is critical that such action steps be clear and explicit. Too often, because of a newfound shared enthusiasm, participants leap into commitments and action steps without taking extra care to confirm them during this final stage. Even though we think we have an understanding, we do not. Later, we are surprised when another person fails to carry out what we had agreed to. The confusion is a result of unclear commitments made during the "Let's Go!" step.

High-Impact Leaders make clear requests regarding actions, with the conditions of satisfaction explicitly stated. Such clarity is crucial because it provides each party to the conversation with an added sense of ownership concerning the commitments involved.

It is important not to force an upward progression along the Tower of Power without building up a solid foundation below. As noted before, you should never skip a step (going from "What's So?" to "Let's Go!", for instance). Nor should you begin the conversation with a step ("What's Possible?", for instance), having neglected earlier necessary steps. Skilled users of the Tower, however, often shift back down to a previous step, depending on the circumstances and quality of the conversation. For example, we might discover at the "What's Possible?" step additional key facts requiring us to move back temporarily to the "What's So?" step. We may feel with "Let's Go!" that the other person's heart and enthusiasm are completely detached from the action steps. This usually indicates that an agenda, want, or need not yet unearthed and revealed remains below the surface, blocking commitment. We would then need to go back and dwell more deliberately on "What's So?" or even "What's Up?" This type of movement is never a waste of time.

USING THE TOWER OF POWER: A CASE STUDY

Ron Stevens, COO and general manager of a global electronics company, was under pressure from the president of the company to deal with a lingering, unresolved problem. Specifically, one of Ron's regional vice presidents was not facing up to a serious issue at the largest plant on the West Coast. Quality at this plant seemed to be slipping, accidents were up, inventory rates continued to accelerate—all of which was increasing warehousing costs in a region simultaneously undergoing a severe budget crunch.

The regional VP, Henry Middleton, seemed stalled with his handling of the plant and the plant manager. It was clear to most people that Henry had to deal with the plant manager in decisive terms. To most observers, removing the plant manager from his position was the obvious solution. Henry had a strong unwillingness to do so, however, and Ron did not feel that it was right to step in and order his direct report to do otherwise. In his mind, it was important to respect Henry as the head of his region, even though none of the actions Henry had taken were providing him with any confidence that the situation would improve. Well known to Ron but unbeknownst to Henry, the president of the company wasn't just dropping hints about the situation anymore; he was losing patience with both of them and demanding action.

I saw this as an opportunity to show how a series of Powerful Conversations could improve, with ripple-like effect, a significant business problem for this company. I coached Ron initially on having a Powerful Conversation with Henry. Then I coached Henry on having a Powerful Conversation with the plant manager. Finally, I guided Henry on having a follow-up Powerful Conversation with Ron. Together, they worked it out and reached the right conclusion. They turned the plant manager's behavior around, and they solved the problem. Production at the plant improved, and the president eased up. Let me illustrate how they got there by recounting one of the Powerful Conversations that took place.

In his initial conversation with Henry, Ron consciously and systematically used the Tower of Power. Because they had had difficulties in their relationship before, Ron felt that he needed a tool to make sure that things stayed on track. He later gave me the following blow-by-blow description of the conversation.

Ron called Henry to headquarters to meet with him. It was apparent to Ron that Henry was aware of the problems and tension associated with the plant, but he did nothing right away to acknowledge the reasons why the meeting was taking place. Ron suspected rightly that Henry's defenses were already on full alert.

After initial small talk, Ron opened discussion around the issues that were concerning him.

> *Ron:* I've been reading reports from the plant in Seattle, Henry, and it's making me feel lost and tremendously frustrated. I can't see what the answers are, yet I'm under pressure from up top to do something now. Anyway, that's what's going on with me around this, and the reason I called you here, but I want to know what's up with you, Henry? How are you feeling about all this?

Henry had been expecting a different and more harsh approach from Ron. He found the tone of Ron's lead-in reassuring. He also quickly related to Ron's concerns.

> *Henry:* I'm frustrated too. And I don't have any immediate answers. It sounds like you're getting beaten up, though. What are they saying?

Ron alluded to the kinds of things the president was concerned about, but he didn't want to get bogged down along those lines. Instead, Ron quickly steered the conversation back to where it concerned Henry most immediately. He asked Henry what was really going on with respect to the plant manager. After all, rumors that the manager would be let go were starting to fly across the region and the company.

> *Henry:* If you want to know the truth, I feel caught in the middle on this. There are a lot of extenuating circumstances going on here and I think Jed, who has been running that plant for a long time, is hanging out there by himself. I feel a lot of loyalty to him and to the work he's done over the years. I just don't think it's right that we dump him over plant problems that are not all completely in his control. It's the way I see us solving a lot of problems these days but it's not how I want to operate.

Ron was taken back a bit himself at this information. It wasn't that he disagreed with Henry's assessment of larger issues. It was that it struck to the heart of some of his own values about what is important, a fact that he promptly relayed to Henry:

> *Ron:* You and I come from the same place on that, Henry. Loyalty is really important to me, too. I'd like to get to the facts of what's going on, then. Let's figure this out.

For the next half hour, Ron and Henry discussed all of the assumptions around problems at the plant. They agreed on five critical factors impacting costs and driving up inventory. As they sorted through these facts, they uncovered a serious issue with sales in the region. In fact, sales forecasts were continually oversupplying production.

Having felt that they had achieved clarity around the "What's So?" of the situation, Ron continued:

> *Ron:* Now that we know what is going on, what do you think the possibilities are? How can we nail down a few options for going forward with some corrective actions? What are your thoughts?

Henry was very responsive to dealing with the facts and options, now that it was clear they were in agreement on all of the circumstances:

> *Henry:* I've given thought to that, believe me. But getting these assumptions down helps me even further. I think we need to pull a team together and I think that this is not an operations issue alone. It has a lot to do with sales and marketing. We have to find a way to get our reporting structure in place and systemize things so we know how much we should be producing each month. It's clear we can't go on the way we are. What do you think we should do to make this happen?

The two men were now fully engaged in the "What's Possible?" stage of the Tower of Power. To this end, Ron discussed some of his experiences in similar cases. It was clearly an opportunity for him to coach Henry about ways he could expand his thinking on the possibilities. Ron recalled some of the strategies used a few years back and he and Henry debated those strategies to find parallels with the current situation.

Moving into the "Let's Go!" stage, Ron checked in with Henry in order to make sure they were getting toward clear commitments:

> *Ron:* Has this helped? What do you need from me in order to get what you need?
>
> *Henry:* What I really need to do is have some way to influence the head of

sales in the region and get him to sign on. Do you have any ideas on how to do that?

They discussed this further and came up with several approaches. Ron went forward to determine their commitments:

Ron: I think I have a lot of valuable information about this. Let's define some clear commitments as to what each of us will do to move forward. Is that okay to do at this point?

Henry: It's exactly what I need.

Henry listed the things that he thought he should do and made proposals to Ron. They each wrote these down, verified them, and agreed on a timetable to get back to each other.

At the end of the session, Ron sought to confirm once more that the conversation had advanced both of their agendas. The two men ended their conversations by reaffirming their commitments:

Ron: I have a lot of information I didn't have before. That's really going to help me out with the president when he asks me about this. For my part, I know exactly what I'm supposed to do. Did you get what you needed in terms of being able to tackle this issue and move us forward?

Henry: I feel good about it too. It's been really helpful to hear about your experiences and ideas and I know what I can do now. I may still run into some glitches, but I'm glad you asked because I feel like I can call you if something comes up that I can't solve.

Ron: You know it. If you e-mail me first thing in the morning I promise I'll get back to you before the end of the day.

Henry: Sold.

They then shook hands and Henry returned to the regional office.

With the meeting over and Henry gone, Ron found himself looking at the Tower of Power on his wall in the office and mentally reviewing what had occurred.

It was all so systematic and clear. He had started with an authentic statement about how he felt. It was simple but candid and it passed the test. He also took the time to check in with Henry about how he was feeling. He credits this alone for getting him past Henry's defensiveness, which had often plagued their prior conversations. Without dwelling too much on what could have been defeatist, Ron moved the conversation past "What's Up?" to "What's So?" and engaged with Henry in a clear analysis of the facts. He was impressed with Henry's insights and understanding and they came to some genuinely surprising conclusions.

Once the facts were established, they worked together to determine the underlying assumptions driving the facts. They did this with clarity and agreement. As leader, Ron was able to coach Henry to see what other issues existed in the data. Together, they were able to move up the Tower to explore the possibilities for action.

At the end, Ron culminated the conversation by checking in to ensure that commitments were clear and Henry had gotten what he needed. Throughout the conversation, Ron felt trust and rapport building between himself and Henry. They had made a genuine connection and would surely be working from a higher platform next time. Ron was looking forward to it.

MEASURING THE IMPACT OF A POWERFUL CONVERSATION

Later, Ron and I analyzed his conversation for impact. Had he successfully used The Tower of Power to produce a Powerful Conversation? We used the three measurements of a Powerful Conversation to find out.

"Are you really sure you had a Powerful Conversation?" I asked. We were joking with each other because he was still elated with his success.

"I'm sure."

"How do you know?"

Ron smiled. "Like certain other important things in life, if you have to ask if you did, then you didn't."

We both laughed.

"Prove it," I said. "A Powerful Conversation advances an agenda, shares learning, and strengthens a relationship. Does yours pass the test?"

Ron grew more serious. "I believe that, at the end of our conversation, Henry was going to go back and attack this problem. That's point one. Point number two is, I learned a heck of a lot about what was going on at that plant. Plus, I have a new agenda of my own to see how we can pull sales and marketing in with operations so that we can go after some higher-level stuff. I realized, for the tenth and hopefully last time, that we need to work in teams with sales and marketing to compete globally."

"What about point three?" I asked.

Ron sat back. "You know, our relationship has always had its ups and downs. Usually when we get into a difficult situation like this, Henry gets defensive, I get angry, he reacts, I get quiet, my patience runs out, and I usually give an order."

"What about this time?"

"I felt that Henry and I worked together in a way that makes me feel a lot better about him than I have in a long time. I saw stuff from him that I haven't seen in 10 years. He has a creative energy that allows him to look at problems in a way none of the other regional VPs come close to. He's quick and I admire that about him. I like being around him because of that."

"How do you think he feels?"

"I imagine he feels pretty good, but I don't know."

We decided that Ron would write a quick e-mail and check in verbally with Henry concerning next steps. He would also make a point of telling Henry that he felt their conversation had actually improved their relationship.

People walk away from a Powerful Conversation feeling energized and positive. That, in itself, is a measurement useful for analyzing its impact. It is not surprising that good feelings emerge when progress has been made in a conversation. Both parties feel that way because they have acknowledged wants and needs and shared ideas. Ultimately, participants in a conversation feel good when agendas have been advanced. High-Impact Leaders certainly feel good when they are able to move forward in ways that positively affect their ability to deliver on results.

The contrast of this is equally revealing. When a conversation has not been genuine and honest, there is nothing positive about the resulting feelings. Energy levels also are reversed. Participants feel tired and drained. Organizations in which Powerful Conversations are not taking place are characterized by low morale and a lack of focus. No one takes charge of an issue. Old patterns stay fixed. We'll talk more about such "bad conversations" in Chapter 4.

For now, keep in mind the positive impact of a Powerful Conversation. Shared learning, building of trust, sincere connection—all of these factors add up to an improved relationship. They also foster environments in which organizations are able to get beyond their defensive routines so that they can really innovate and create value. There is nothing more liberating, satisfying, or motivating than when individuals in an organization are able to collaborate successfully in realizing vision and strategy.

At the end of a Powerful Conversation, memories of frustrations and tiredness are gone. Only the energy remains. And that is the energy that fuels great achievements.

CHAPTER 3

THE TYPES OF POWERFUL CONVERSATIONS

HIGH-IMPACT LEADERS are focused and targeted in the way they use Powerful Conversations. They recognize that Powerful Conversations, while always worthwhile, are time consuming and demanding. So High-Impact Leaders use Powerful Conversations in specific ways and with specific objectives in mind in order to move work forward. In this chapter, I want to show you how they do this. First, though, we need to understand better the critical knowledge, skills, and abilities that underlie the success of a High-Impact Leader.

THE COMPETENCIES OF HIGH-IMPACT LEADERS

Warren Bennis, author of *On Becoming a Leader* and founder of the Leadership Institute at the University of Southern California, is a close personal friend. He is also my cochair at Linkage's annual Global Institute for Leadership Development and a partner in the research we have conducted to examine the traits and characteristics of High-Impact Leaders. I don't know anyone else who has done more to advance the understanding of what leadership is and how leadership capability is developed.

Working closely together in recent years, Warren and I have found that, despite the tremendous variety and diversity in the personalities of great leaders, important commonalties exist around certain traits and behaviors. In an attempt to analyze, understand, and demystify the art of leadership, we have developed a model to capture the critical ingredients of high-performance leadership and an assessment instrument based on that model: the Leadership Assessment Instrument (LAI). A self-scoring sample of the items on the LAI is included in the Appendix of this book. I encourage you to take a close look at how the instrument works. By taking the LAI yourself, you will have a clearer understanding of your own leadership abilities. An understanding of your own competency profile will provide a strong base on which to build on your skills further as a High-Impact Leader.

The LAI tests for the five competencies we identified in our research (Focused Drive, Emotional Intelligence, Trusted Influence, Conceptual Thinking, and Systems Thinking). These are the building blocks of high-performance leadership. Each has two components. The competency of Focused Drive, for example, requires the proper mix of both focus and drive. Ample focus but not enough drive won't produce many results; plenty of drive but little focus, on the other hand, often fails to produce the right results. But if a leader has both focus and drive—and can balance them well—he or she will be able to achieve high performance through Focused Drive.

Thousands of leaders have used the LAI to assess and develop their leadership competencies. Their results paint a scientific portrait of the essence of leadership. Significantly, the picture the LAI draws of one leader is always somewhat different from that of another. This is consistent with common experience. High-Impact Leaders, after all, come in all shapes and forms. Some are quiet and introverted, while others are bold, outgoing, and charismatic; some lead by action, others through vision. In addition, we have observed that during multirater assessments (i.e., when the evaluation of peers and those working for a leader are included), High-Impact Leaders consistently and inevitably rate themselves lower than others do. This speaks not only to the humility of High-Impact Leaders, but also to a finely tuned awareness of their own weaknesses. This evidences yet another common characteristic of High-Impact Leaders: they all want to grow and are always pushing themselves further and further past their limits.

THE TYPES OF POWERFUL CONVERSATIONS

At bottom, leaders *actualize strategy* through conversations around Focused Drive. They *stabilize* through conversations around Emotional Intelligence. They *build trust* through their conversations around Trusted

Influence. They *drive ideas* through conversations around Conceptual Thinking. And they *systemize* and focus work processes through conversations around Systems Thinking. You can break it down to finer detail, or slap different labels on these tasks, but you will find that at the end of the day, this remains the essence of a High-Impact Leader's work.

There are, then, five primary types of Powerful Conversations: those that actualize strategy, those that stabilize, those that build trust, those that drive ideas, and those that systemize. Each calls for and is based upon one of the leadership competencies we identified in our research. Each is critical for a High-Impact Leader to master in order to advance his or her agenda, foster learning, and strengthen relationships.

A High-Impact Leader's use of Powerful Conversations, as well as his or her tendency to rely on certain types of Powerful Conversations vis-à-vis others, stems directly from his or her competency profile. All High-Impact Leaders try to maximize their strengths by engaging in certain types of Powerful Conversations. Let's see how by examining each of the five primary types of Powerful Conversations.

Actualizing Strategy Through Focused Drive

Imagine you have to go to your high school reunion. How does this make you feel?

I love to ask this question because of the intensity of the reactions that emerge. For most of us, the thought of revisiting our high school days creates anxiety or sometimes even outright fear. And why not? What a pressure of expectations and worries this can set up! The prevailing question is always, "Who has really made it?" And it invariably turns out that the most successful members of a high school class are not the ones who were necessarily the smartest or the most charismatic or even the ones who had the most potential. Rather, the people who accomplish the most in life and are considered successful are frequently those who are the most focused and driven. They are the ones with the competency of Focused Drive.

Focused Drive is a balance between focus and drive. *Focus* is the ability to maintain attention on key issues despite disruptions. A focused person will target initiatives requiring special attention and display single-mindedness in directing energy. *Drive* is characterized by acting decisively to make things happen. A driven person strives for ambitious goals rather than the safety of achievable results and has a willingness to do whatever it takes to get things done, displaying stamina and energy over the long term. High-Impact Leaders are leaders not only because they themselves are focused and driven but because they are able to generate this kind of energy and motivation in those around them. They use Powerful Conversations that actualize strategy to do so.

Communication that instills Focused Drive is a complex package. Instilling focus is a matter of defining a simple and clear goal for the organization out of the immeasurably vast and complex sea of issues, pressures, and possibilities. The companion step is to determine and communicate the steps that are necessary to reach that goal. Instilling drive involves creating a sense in others of the urgency, necessity, and determination (as well as the capability) to accomplish that goal—in other words, motivating others to take the steps to actualize a goal. Enthusiasm, energy, persistence, clarity, and reward are the elements of conversations that High-Impact Leaders use to influence those around them to actualize strategy.

This is really about being a trailblazer. When confusion, disorder, or disorganization reigns, the High-Impact Leader is the one who channels emotion and activity toward objectives, setting a path for others to follow. This is most clearly and dramatically observed during periods of crisis or danger.

In reality, all organizations are mere days, months, or quarters away from crisis. The work of the High-Impact Leader is to set a clear purpose, establish vision, and focus the organization on the day-to-day steps necessary to actualize strategy. It is not difficult to think of great leaders who have responded to a crisis and communicated to others in a way that instilled them with Focused Drive. Think of Winston Churchill motivating a surrounded and resource-scarce nation to never surrender and to focus on, and drive toward, victory. More recently, consider how George Bush used the telephone to build a coalition of diverse interests during the Gulf War, employing his own Focused Drive to create focus and drive in others.

These were dramatic political events that played themselves out on the world stage. Don't be fooled into thinking that this type of Powerful Conversation can only happen at a place like Downing Street or Pennsylvania Avenue. In fact, Powerful Conversations involving the actualization of strategy happen every day in business. Consider the following success story.

Shortly after Senior Vice President June Rokoff became responsible for a vital product release at Lotus Development Corporation, she learned that she had inherited a crisis situation. The development team was up against an "undoable" schedule to deliver the product and morale was at rock bottom. Recognizing that incredible Focused Drive was needed, Rokoff rallied the troops and overcame all odds to deliver a great product, one that has become legendary in the computer world. How did she do it?

Upon taking command of the project and learning of the situation, her first response was to gather everyone together for an honest, open discussion. There was much airing of frustration and blame about the situation. Rokoff advanced the dialogue with an expression of her own fears and was able to win over her team to get its members to tell her in great detail about the facts and drivers of the problems that they faced. Together, and with candor, they started to identify some solutions to their problems.

For an individual to be focused and driven is one thing; it is much more challenging—and important—to instill that sense of focused, must-do urgency in others, especially in those who are anticipating and resigned to failure. As a High-Impact Leader, Rokoff used her skill with words to inspire her team with a challenge. Of equal importance, she bolstered credibility in her vision with realistic clarity about the efforts the challenge would require. She also supported her words with her own efforts and promises. And she committed to supporting the team with whatever it needed to knock down obstacles. Where bureaucracy and a "can't-do" attitude stood in her way, she led her team to find ways to go over, around, or through those hurdles.

Rokoff knew this kind of Focused Drive would require support not only from within the organization but from outside as well. She was wise enough to turn to her team's families to solicit further support. She wrote notes to each family in order to explain the circumstances and importance of their task and to thank them in advance for their commitment in supporting such a difficult challenge involving so much time away from home. She let them know that this period would not last forever and she promised rewards at the end of the tunnel.

In sum, for June Rokoff and her team at Lotus, every day became a series of Powerful Conversations concerning needs, commitments, and goals. The dialogue was so strong it rippled outward to customers, suppliers, shareholders, and even family members of the team. It serves as a model of actualizing strategy through Focused Drive.

Consider the contrast with another leader and organization with whom I became acquainted some time ago. The president of this large company, facing a crisis situation in an extremely competitive market, needed to increase quality and productivity at the same time. Gathering his senior team for a key meeting, he announced the solution to their problems. "Within the next two quarters we must, in order to maintain our market share, increase our throughput by 10 percent and reduce our recall by half its current number. I have the utmost confidence in everyone in this room to accomplish this."

It may seem that this leader's statement modeled and instilled Focused Drive. In fact, it was unfocused and demotivating. Without acknowledging underlying problems or circumstances, without opening the floor to an honest discussion of concerns, worries, issues, and fears, the president alone set the agenda. This resulted in everyone paying lip service to his goals. He did not give them steps or commitments for achieving the goals. And he further widened the gap between reality and optimism by expressing confidence that was completely unsupported by an expression of understanding of underlying factors. Imagine the difference in focus and energy if this president had opened the floor to emotions and facts, developed clear commitments, and given his team a vision it could buy into and follow wholeheartedly.

High-Impact Leaders use Focused Drive to actualize strategy. Such Powerful Conversations clarify the situation and motivate the participants. Each such conversation begins with a clear statement that sets a purpose and goal. It defines clearly for the individual the part he or she needs to play, asks the individual what he or she needs and wants in order to accomplish that goal, and stresses the importance of driving toward that goal. This is the way a leader makes goals happen. This is the way a leader actualizes strategy.

Stabilizing Through Emotional Intelligence

Much light has been shed recently on the role of Emotional Intelligence in human society and work. Books by Daniel Goleman and others have furthered our understanding of the kind of intelligence that functions well interpersonally. As common experience indicates, neither IQ nor formal education is a valid indicator of success in the real world. They certainly don't hurt, but by the same token, a high IQ or a degree from a top-flight business school doesn't guarantee success. There is another factor in the mix—Emotional Intelligence, or EQ—that dictates how well we get along with others and respond to the assortment of influences and issues we face on any given day.

Emotional Intelligence is a balance between perception and emotional maturity. *Perception* involves a consideration of the feelings of others, taking into account differences in personal makeup and the impact of emotions and feelings as well as psychological and emotional needs. *Emotional maturity* involves an ability to control and filter emotions in a constructive way. All told, High-Impact Leaders with Emotional Intelligence tend to possess sincerity, empathy, humility, optimism, and determination. They exhibit these traits through Powerful Conversations that are stabilizing in nature. These are the conversations that calm stressful situations and provide grounded hope for optimistic outcomes.

High-Impact Leaders use Emotional Intelligence to stabilize stressful situations. This type of Powerful Conversation involves perceiving and recognizing the true feelings of others; maintaining emotional balance despite anxiety and fear; and moving individuals away from inaction toward hope and optimism. Those with high EQs are frequently unfazed by what would cause most of us to collapse in inaction, distress, or panic. This is primarily because they are able to compartmentalize their own feelings and rationalize assessments, but also because they are able to channel stress into positive energy.

Because they are intrinsically and overwhelmingly optimistic and action oriented, High-Impact Leaders are great handlers of, if not thrivers on, stress. They are the quickest to recognize the positive potentials behind difficult situations. What would burden so many of us is a game to great leaders; many of them talk about the fun of it all.

High-Impact Leaders believe in their ability to ride out storms, but have the empathy to acknowledge and understand the fears of others. A High-Impact Leader cannot create widespread optimism without doing this first. This is difficult for many High-Impact Leaders because, being people of great optimism, they are willing and able to race ahead of their followers toward positive action. The recipe for a stabilizing Powerful Conversation, though, calls for an initial recognition of fear and anxiety. If these are not recognized, they will never be alleviated.

Leaders frequently tell people around them to "stop worrying." But High-Impact Leaders know that you cannot command a person not to worry. They recognize the positive aspects of worry. Indeed, worry creates the possibility for preemptive action. Worry helps to pinpoint problems. Worry becomes the foundation for problem solving. Treated positively, worry is a method for probing and compartmentalizing underlying facts and assumptions. On the other hand, hope is the ability to see the optimistic possibilities inherent in any bad situation and to convey that optimism to others. Hope overcomes worry through acknowledgment and by painting a picture of opportunity or possibility. Think again of Winston Churchill or Franklin Roosevelt confronting the overwhelming fears of war and turning that into action and victory.

John Keane at Keane, Inc. faced such worry and fear in the early 1980s when the performance of his company dipped. Facing this tremendous disappointment, Keane gathered his executive team and listened to a list of contributing problems that were external to the organization and, consequently, that much more frustrating to such an action-oriented team. Efforts at expanding the customer base were an uphill battle against the forces of a recession, and economic forecasters saw no upturn in sight. Even worse was the frustration of knowing that the organization, unlike many of its competitors, had been doing things right and had executed its game plan flawlessly. Now, factors beyond its immediate control were hampering Keane's best-laid plans.

If John Keane had been a leader without Emotional Intelligence, he might have responded differently—with an emotional outburst, a blast of temper, a bombastic threat, or some other sign of low EQ. Instead, John Keane acknowledged the difficulties faced by the organization and painted a different picture. He likened the situation to a sailboat race when the wind has stopped. The lack of wind affects everyone equally. All the sails are flapping and there seems to be nothing to do but sit and wait. Keane painted a different picture: "The best teams spend their time and energy getting the boat ready so that when the wind picks up again, they are the first to catch it. It's not misfortune we are facing but a great chance."

Keane's optimism reassured his team and the entire organization. With hope as the team's guidepost, the real task at hand was now to take the steps necessary to prepare for moving fast when the wind returned. The team coalesced around defining what those steps were and determining how to take them. From a time of despair and hopelessness emerged a sense of motivated commitment, possibility, and reward.

Being a High-Impact Leader, Keane took this even further. He gave his team a look into the future by predicting that this sort of crisis would occur again. He told them that the tide comes in and the tide goes out, and when the tide is out, you can see the rocks. The organization would be smarter, more flexible, and more prepared to move from fear to positive action if it understood this cycle in advance. Keane was so masterful at employing the stabilizing type of Powerful Conversation that he not only calmed the crisis, but also infused his management team—and the organization—with a stability and unshakable confidence in their ability to weather future storms.

True to John Keane's word, when the economy rebounded and the wind came back several years later, the sailboat at Keane, Inc. was in better shape than the other boats in the race. The organization has never looked back, becoming one of the best shareholder performing companies in the twentieth century.

Building Trust Through Trusted Influence

At Linkage's 1997 Global Institute for Leadership Development, a panel of distinguished CEOs (Bob Galvin of Motorola, Bob Haas of Levi Strauss, and Max DePree of Herman Miller) met to discuss the lessons of leadership. When asked what fundamental truth of management has remained unaltered by the coming and going of fads and theories over the years, the panel was in full agreement: trust was the constant. Galvin stated that he considered trust to be the greatest motivator in an organization. DePree added that "trust takes a lot of moxie and commitment to build. It takes a long time, and you can lose it overnight."

The competency of *Trusted Influence* is a balance between commitment and empowerment. *Commitment* involves aligning shared goals with shared values. *Empowerment* is about displaying trust in others by delegating responsibility and inviting participation in decision making. Great leaders are exciting to be around because they create winning scenarios. The high expectations they have of others, complemented with empathy and commitment about needs, create this sense of confidence and enablement.

Great coaches are examples of those who promote loyalty and trust in order to achieve specific, directed objectives. Consider Bill Parcells, who has served as the head coach of three different NFL football teams—the New York Giants, the New England Patriots, and the New York Jets. Each of these teams was hopeless when Parcells assumed the reins; each has risen to Super Bowl contention almost immediately under his guidance. Parcells is legendary for creating overnight success, and yet the makeup of each of his teams shows that success has been anything but overnight. In reality, each time Parcells has moved to a new team, a core group of assistant coaches has moved with him. As Dennis Green, head coach of the Minnesota Vikings, says, "No one truly knows what goes on behind those closed doors, but outside, you can see that Bill coached a few years and then he left the game. And then when he came back, those same assistants went running to be back with him. That tells you something. It's respect. It's called working conditions."

The competency of Trusted Influence, then, lies at the heart of Bill Parcells' success. He earns the fierce loyalty and commitment of his assistant coaches by cultivating shared goals about how football should be played (in hard-hitting style, with an emphasis on fundamentals) and why it should be played in such a fashion (to win Super Bowls). Parcells backs up this commitment with action, making sure his coaches are well compensated and internally recognized for the overall success of the team. And he empowers them. For example, Parcells gives Bill Belichick, his longtime defensive coordinator, free reign to engineer the defensive schemes, as long as they remain with the parameters of Parcells' overall philosophy. Belichick has become acknowledged as a defensive genius and has had several opportunities to become head coach of his own team. Unsurprisingly, Belichick—like the rest of Bill Parcells' loyal cadre of assistant coaches—has elected to remain firmly by his mentor's side.

Powerful Conversations involving Trusted Influence have three legs of support: (1) saying what you are going to do clearly and doing it consistently; (2) demonstrating a true sense of caring; and (3) expressing and sharing beliefs in nonjudgmental ways. Above all, leaders need to be aware that they are making explicit and implicit commitments on a day-to-day basis. Clarity is required, or else impression and interpretation are up for grabs. Even unintentional promises carry weight and affect loyalty. Think back to Mike Ruettgers, the president of EMC Corporation who carries a notebook to keep a journal of his conversations and track his promises. In doing so, Ruettgers also sends a clear message to others that his commitments are serious.

Caring is another way to develop Trusted Influence. It is important for leaders to pay attention to "satisfiers" and check in periodically with people about these satisfiers. High-Impact Leaders also take the time and energy to know the people around them. They remember their families and the things that impact their lives. I know of no better way to show caring than to acknowledge the life and impact points of others.

Finally, while being true to his or her own beliefs is vital for a leader in order to develop Trusted Influence, it is equally important to recognize and respect the perspectives of others in a nonjudgmental fashion. High-Impact Leaders accept the reasonable variances, customs, and beliefs of a diverse society. Flexibility is at a premium for leaders today. In a diverse world, demonstrating caring can be a challenge. It also creates a tremendous opportunity for learning, as well as a chance to grow relationships.

The following story illustrates how High-Impact Leaders employ Trusted Influence in their Powerful Conversations. In the early days of Linkage, with only a few dedicated people, some small accounts, lots of drive, and a few good ideas, we needed help in meeting our ambitious goals. I hired a coach to guide us along and ensure we were doing all the right things. I got so much more than I expected.

Mike Davis had grown Watson Wyatt from a small organization to a worldwide powerhouse with 4500 employees and $700 million in annual revenues. He had recently retired and was doing research at Harvard. I felt that his experience of developing and growing a start-up would help alert us to what we would be facing. It was, more specifically, his ability to give us those feelings of confidence and enablement that were his critical contribution to the early success of Linkage. Through Powerful Conversations, he made us feel as if we had the greatest ideas in the world and could carry them out. He made a big deal about our plans. He got excited about our challenges. He listened to our smallest worries. And he somehow made us believe in what we were doing.

When I found out that Mike had cancer, I was shocked because he had never spoken about it. Mike discouraged any discussion of his condition, dismissing the illness as something that would blow over. One particular Friday, on a day when his health appeared even worse, Mike and I had a conversation that really impacted me. We talked about the true core of my fears around making Linkage a successful company. "Don't worry, Phil," he reassured me. "You are ahead of the curve. You have better processes than my company had at a similar stage. You are going to win. Besides, look at how much fun you're having!" He moved me beyond my concerns to show me an optimistic future.

I called Mike after the weekend and found out that his condition had worsened. On Tuesday, he died. I sat and cried at the realization that this man had spent the Friday before helping us along. His funeral was attended by hundreds of his former employees, peers, customers, and competitors. Time after time that day, people would go to the podium to relate personal incidents of how Mike had touched them and helped them along. Everyone, it seemed, had had a similar experience with Mike. I heard enough stories that day to fill two books.

A High-Impact Leader like Mike Davis, who uses Powerful Conversations to develop confidence and bring out the best in others, will receive high levels of trust and loyalty in return. So many leaders want to secure trust, but they can't get there automatically. The clear pathway is to engage in Powerful Conversations that build trust.

Driving Ideas Through Conceptual Thinking

In my estimation, Gary Hamel is the leading thinker on strategy and innovation today. He argues that organizations that want to thrive in today's rapidly changing economy will have to learn how to harness the passion and imagination of every employee in the quest for strategy innovation. It's not just a matter of competing well in the same market with the same competitors and conditions anymore; it's about competing in markets that haven't even been imagined yet. If this is true—and I believe Hamel to be right—it necessitates a revolution in how we uncover ideas inside organizations. High-Impact Leaders rely on Conceptual Thinking and Powerful Conversations that drive ideas for these purposes.

Conceptual Thinking is a balance between innovation and big picture thinking. *Innovation* involves seeking better solutions to problems, testing assumptions, challenging the status quo, and improving on ideas in ways that create profit or growth potential. *Big picture thinking* is characterized by an ability to conceptualize underlying or systemic causes driving a problem or issue. Big picture thinkers make connections between and among data and events in ways that reveal key issues or opportunities. They are able to interpret ambiguous circumstances or information and have an intuitive ability to clarify possibilities.

Ideas can no longer be the prerogative of the leadership team alone. In a world where customer intimacy (i.e., an accurate understanding of customer needs and wants) is the main driver for strategic innovation, a leadership team may in fact be the last to gain exposure to a revolutionary new idea. Today's High-Impact Leaders must build an organization that allows innovation to rise to the surface and is unencumbered by level, title, or the status quo.

It is impossible to do this without trust and openness, as well as the respect and honesty that travels with those qualities. Think again of Digital Equipment Corporation—market leader one instant, acquisition target the next. Similar miscues have occurred countless times. Xerox allowed Steve Jobs to walk out the door, along with his concepts for user-friendly operating systems. General Motors handed its supremacy in the truck business over to Ford while engaged in its own internal battles on the production line. Barnes & Noble, striving for market share measured in territory and bookstores, didn't see Amazon.com going after access and distribution. Pan Am and other major U.S. carriers ignored the customer and slept while People's Express invented a new model of service and price competitiveness. Though People's Express failed in the end, Southwest Airlines learned from those mistakes and is now cleaning up.

High-Impact Leaders use Powerful Conversations to build a climate of learning where all assumptions are challenged, all employees are empowered, and open dialogue reigns. In such an organization, learning is radically increased because every occasion is a chance to exchange valuable information around facts and assumptions. Tough questions are asked. Better solutions are actively sought. Defenses or egos that might have made sacred cows or ways of business undiscussable are no longer barriers. Rapport between colleagues up and down the ranks expedites the leaps toward the connections, synergies, and new ideas that are the fundamentals of the innovative organization. Because Powerful Conversations focused on driving ideas unleash learning and challenge assumptions, they are a tremendous source of energy. Nothing is more exciting or more powerful than an idea that has just come to light. It is like finding gold while shoveling dirt.

Any High-Impact Leader striving to achieve a great idea must also engage the full support, energy, passion, feedback, and brain power of the organization's employees. To this end, it is vital for a High-Impact Leader to express strong feelings around his or her big picture goals through Powerful Conversations in order to lift others beyond their immediate concerns. Think of John Kennedy and the way he articulated his vision of a man on the moon. Despite the daily crises of the Cold War and a host of ongoing domestic issues, Kennedy was able to look ahead and see the possibilities—and the importance—of a moon landing. It is firm evidence of his leadership that he was able to get the rest of the country to focus in a similar long-range, big-picture fashion.

In everyday business, a High-Impact Leader uses simple but powerful metaphors to instill the big picture in many people spread throughout an organization. You must express a great need for support in order to receive support for that vision. This may seem obvious, but too often leaders about to engage in a journey toward a bold goal disempower and demotivate others by not impressing upon them the need for their support. But the leader cannot force that support. Goals cannot be ordained or declared by decree. Clearly defining facts and openly questioning underlying assumptions ensures a movement toward the big picture, no matter how audacious. Here again, we see the importance of flexibility: a leader must be willing to fine-tune the big picture based on the feedback of others. Similarly, the leader cannot blindly assume that the fine-tuned big picture will develop without perspiration. There is nothing less empowering and more defeating than seeking goals without recognizing or at least acknowledging the challenges that lie ahead.

High-Impact Leaders use Conceptual Thinking to drive ideas. Such Powerful Conversations release the individuals in an organization from the constraints of hierarchical thinking and free them from following down the same old paths, taking the organization in exciting new directions.

Systemizing Through Systems Thinking

Systemizing Powerful Conversations are those that focus on how work gets done in an organization. High-Impact Leaders use them to create organized Systems Thinking about the processes and work practices of the organization.

Systems Thinking is a balance between process orientation and mental discipline. *Process orientation* involves taking steps to ensure that new ideas are integrated with established procedures. People skilled in this area are able to perceive the organization in terms of critical and highly interrelated work processes. They are also adept at identifying the right people necessary to make a project work. *Mental discipline* is about displaying rigor in thinking through difficult situations. It calls for deliberate and systematic steering through ambiguity and cluttered information.

Systemizing Powerful Conversations usually examine the fundamentals of doing work. They involve an open and honest analysis of situations, goals, and expected outcomes. This may sound like a natural occurrence within organizations, but in my experience, it is quite rare. What usually happens is that the leader does not open him- or herself up to this honest analysis and proceeds as soon as possible to the "Let's Go!" stage of a conversation.

Consider, for example, one of the world's oldest family-run steel businesses. A while back, the company was faced with the challenge of increasing its spare parts sales while maintaining a tight cost reduction effort. During the initial strategy meeting, quick assessments led to the following knee-jerk recommendations: (1) more training of the sales force to increase sales, (2) more incentive for the sales force to expand revenue targets, and (3) more tracking of the number of sales calls per month to measure effectiveness. In fact, these recommendations were off base. It was only through a series of Powerful Conversations that real needs were uncovered and an effective plan was formulated.

I facilitated a series of meetings with 10 representatives from around the organization. In those sessions, a surprising amount of emotion was expressed concerning current sales efforts. There was a general frustration at not being able to access salespeople when needed. Some asserted a position that "sales through a traditional sales force" was a game the organization should no longer play, that in fact other routes would be more effective. Others felt that the sales force, though useful, had been exalted into overpaid, prima donna status.

Advancing this discussion, real needs were discussed:

1. The sales force needed to call directly on fewer accounts and be more available to work inside the organization with field engineers.
2. Sales managers needed more direct leads from field engineers and others with customer contact.
3. Leaders representing internal functions needed better communication, including updated files on accounts, so that during customer site visits, all information was available.

An open examination of facts led to these agreements:

1. The sales organization was selling up to capacity with current staffing and training.

2. Sales capacity could be increased tenfold by focusing on developing the sales skills of field engineers—those in the most direct contact with the customer.

3. Staff at the customer service call center could also be trained to identify and develop sales leads.

After reaching this level of understanding around needs, assumptions, and facts, it was easy to move on to committed action. Specifically, the leadership team agreed to:

1. Create direct marketing efforts inside the organization with current service personnel.

2. Develop a lead generation system that recognized and rewarded those who contributed leads.

3. Include online record keeping as a task of the sales staff in order to increase the quality and timeliness of information available to all within the company when dealing with a customer.

Out of this systemized approach came a very different and more effective strategy for the organization—quite unlike the one that would have resulted if the initial recommendations had been adopted. Rather than focusing on improving training for 30 sales force staff members, training was instead directed at the 200 field engineers and 70 customer service call center representatives. Information tracking was made a priority. A lead generation system was established.

The goal of these committed efforts was set at increasing spare part sales by 30 percent a year over three years. The company blew this goal away. At the end of three years, spare part sales had increased by 153 percent.

In sum, High-Impact Leaders use Powerful Conversations strategically to achieve their goals. Our analysis of the five types of Powerful Conversations provides a clearer picture of the deliberate intent behind a leader's communication within the organization. Of course, conversations in real life may seem a muddled mixture. They may and do take place not just in structured meetings and through scripted speeches, but also on the run and in hallways. The High-Impact Leaders that I have observed, however, exhibit conscious forethought about who they want to talk with and why, as well as what ends they want to achieve through their interactions. They plan and use the different types of Powerful Conversations to maximize their impact.

THE SWAMP: GETTING INTO AND OUT OF BAD CONVERSATIONS

ENGAGING IN A Powerful Conversation brings the participants to a higher place in an expedited way. A Powerful Conversation really has power: it's exhilarating, it's deeply connecting, and it drives results.

But we all know how destructive a conversation can be when things go wrong or when two people fail to see eye to eye. We've all gotten stuck in conversations that go nowhere or cause bad feelings to erupt—conversations that leave people exhausted, distrustful, or just plain frustrated. The blame for that type of conversation can hardly ever be attributed solely to one person or the other. In most instances, the blame is shared (although that may be the only thing that is shared). In this chapter, we will look at where bad conversations go wrong and what happens when they do. We will also examine how a bad conversation can be turned around and put back on track toward positive results.

Bad conversations are tremendously damaging to individuals and organizations. Even more clearly than Powerful Conversations, bad conversations seem to ripple from micro to macro levels, transferring from the individuals involved to infect those around them in ways that negatively impact the energy, culture, and teamwork of a group. Bad conversations with customers can affect a company's bottom line and result in poor relationships and lost business. Even more serious than the immediate damage of a bad conversation is the cost of lost opportunity and lost effectiveness.

In our study of Powerful Conversations, a look at bad conversations is an important way for us to examine how conversations function. It highlights the ways we can work toward solutions, despite difficult circumstances, through Powerful Conversations—not bad conversations.

POWERFUL CONVERSATIONS VERSUS BAD CONVERSATIONS

How draining a bad conversation can be. As soon as I think of one, I am reminded of the resulting loss of energy, the bad feelings, the sense of wasted time, and, indeed, the wasted opportunity. It is amazing how a negative interaction can stay with us long after the fact. Personally, a bad conversation can plague and haunt me night and day. I find myself going over and over it in my head, thinking about the righteousness of my position and the wrongs I felt. I try to shake it off, but it won't go away.

In contrast, a Powerful Conversation is always energizing. Even the most mentally exhausting conversation or meeting, if it is powerful, results in an exhilarating feeling. The memory of such an experience obscures the lethargic and tiring parts. You are left with an optimistic energy; you look forward to the next opportunity to meet or talk. In a Powerful Conversation, there is a sensation often described as a "click." Good things begin to happen. Ideas begin to flow. The relationship gets stronger, even with someone you barely know. There is lasting impact. Goals are achieved.

None of this happens with bad conversations, which are destructive and emotionally draining. There is no replenishment after such an experience. Indeed, you are lucky if you are able to forget it at all. I look back on a bad conversation and say, "How did I let that happen? Why did I say what I did?" I chide myself for letting my emotions or bad tendencies get ahead of my reason, logic, and discipline.

In short, a bad conversation is exactly the opposite of a Powerful Conversation. While I offer no pithy definition of bad conversations, I assure you that you know when you're involved in one. In case there is any doubt, you can also hearken back to the three measurements of a Powerful Conversation (advanced agenda, shared learning, deepened relationship), because a bad conversation produces absolutely nothing in these regards.

Agenda

In a bad conversation, an agenda is not advanced. Moreover, if progress has previously been made on any goals or objectives, a bad conversation can reverse that progress. Indeed, participants in a bad conversation may even go so far as to deny or fail to remember commitments that have been made and assumptions that have been agreed to prior to entering "the Swamp" (a place that I will describe more fully later in the chapter).

As an example, I recently observed a sales meeting at Linkage quickly lose its focus on agendas when problems emerged and complaints grew louder than goals. The meeting had been scheduled to kick off the attendee sales efforts for one of our yearly programs. The leaders of the meeting— the program managers—were making their presentation to the sales force and had succeeded in large measure in getting the salespeople excited about what was a very strong event with specific and detailed selling points.

Then someone grumbled about the timing of the program. Having the program fall between Thanksgiving and Christmas every year was a consistent mistake, he said. Every member of the sales force had his or her own private grievance about losing a significant sale for this program because of its inconvenient timing. Once unleashed, the stories became a tidal wave, overruling all the progress that had already been made. The program managers, while sympathetic to some degree, became more and more frustrated and angry. The situation threatened to become a real problem.

Then a small voice spoke up as if from nowhere. The Midwest office sales rep was listening in on the meeting by conference call. No one had remembered that she was there when the conversation degenerated. Her voice was a surprise.

"Look, I have a question," she said.

Everyone listened.

"I don't see how this discussion has any value at all. I'm out here in the regional office and I feel like I'm all by myself. I thought we were going to share closing techniques to get more sales, not to discuss what's wrong with the schedule. You guys are around each other all the time. Can we please refocus on how we are going to achieve our goals? I really need this information to make my numbers."

Chastened, sharing a guilty laugh, the group was knocked out of its downward spiral and got back to work. We had sunk into the Swamp and hadn't known it.

Learning

In a bad conversation, points are made, explanations offered, and facts argued, but information is not shared and learning is not advanced. This may be because each participant is locked into a rigid point of view or is perhaps discussing a completely distinct matter from the other participants.

Defensive routines often override any chance of unearthing new thinking. At other times, information sharing is prevented and learning impeded by simple actions such as talking when another person is speaking or by behavioral attitudes such as giving over to emotional outbursts, resorting to blame, excuse, recrimination, and so on. About the only thing people learn in a bad conversation is that they don't want to be in one again.

Relationships

As a result of a bad conversation, relationships are not advanced and are more often than not harmed. The resulting bad feelings for another person can reduce levels of trust and damage rapport. When conversations are extremely negative and when those patterns of behavior become fixed, a relationship may become irrevocably damaged. In the heat of a bad conversation, people say things that might never be forgiven or even forgotten. At the very least, it can take a tremendous amount of time and emotional effort to rebuild a relationship damaged by a very bad conversation. The journey back is usually painful and slow.

I offer another example drawn from Linkage. A development meeting was scheduled for 1 P.M. on a Wednesday, involving several senior officers and senior program directors. A client had called me with an emergency that morning and I was late. The vice president of programs was also late for some other reason. Coincidentally, we both joined the meeting at the same time, nearly one hour after it had started.

The meeting participants had been trying to wrestle a conceptual issue to the ground for more than an hour and were disappointed that we had not been there to provide our input. As soon as we walked in, one program director made a comment that showed his anger. Trying to express his honest feelings, he said: "I'm mad that you guys weren't here. This is an important meeting. I really rely on you two in particular for your conceptual thinking." This set off a chain reaction of feelings in the room. Those who had been involved in the meeting from the beginning felt insulted. The vice president was defensive about the reasons why he was late. I was feeling angry. We were suddenly mired in the Swamp.

If we had tried to push forward anyway, I think something bad might have happened, perhaps even something irreparable. Someone spoke up, however, and suggested that we stop the meeting right then, despite the fact that we were all finally gathered. He offered the suggestion that we get together on Saturday morning for a fresh start. It was the right thing to do under the circumstances.

I offer the example to show how quickly things can sometimes turn around. Even when you are conscious of bad conversations and how they manifest themselves, it doesn't make it any easier to be rational when emotions and strong feelings begin to clash. When we reconvened on Saturday, emotions had cooled and we were no longer in the Swamp. With honest feelings and without hidden dialogue, we used the Tower of Power to forge a solid "Let's Go!" strategy.

THE SOURCE OF BAD CONVERSATIONS

Even the most powerful communicators can't completely escape from bad conversations. We all have our moments of irrationality, obtuseness, obstinance, emotional outbursts, self-pity, and blame, and we all can be guilty of manipulation and willful destructiveness. These are the characteristics that underlie and contribute to bad conversations. It is important to realize that bad conversations can come in intentional and unintentional forms, and that we can be guilty of either at different times.

Conversations that become bad in unintentional ways are usually characterized by a lack of skill in communicating or a temporary lack of understanding of the tenets of Powerful Conversations. Misinterpretation, lack of patience, and poor sharing of emotions or true feelings can unintentionally—and quickly—lead you into the Swamp. Unintentional bad conversations are often those that disintegrate during their course. Things start okay and deteriorate. Meanings are lost, perspectives are distorted, and defensiveness rises. What is said does not match what was intended. Clarity is poor. Nonverbal signals can contradict verbal ones. Values, cultures, and norms of behavior often clash.

A skilled conversationalist can recognize these warning signs and take appropriate steps to reduce or reverse this negative slide. In many cases, however, unintentional bad conversations leave all parties shaking their heads and unable to recognize or work out where things went wrong. Facilitators help because they can observe traits and behaviors. Practice and care can reduce the likelihood of dysfunctional traits and behaviors being exhibited.

Characteristics of bad conversations include:

- Unclear, poorly expressed, or poorly understood content
- Unfocused content marked by tangents, or the cramming in of too many facts, concerns, wants, and needs
- Frequent interruptions leading to poor exchange of signals and information as well as rising frustration
- Uninterested participation and lack of active listening

- Unexpressed feelings or beliefs, guarded emotions, and unspoken needs and wants
- Indirect language, with facts and assumptions ineffectively communicated
- Harsh voice and tone, often unintentionally at odds with message
- Nonverbal signs at odds with words, revealing true negative feelings
- Unresponsive body language, such as poor eye contact, turning away, and crossed arms

THE OUTPUTS OF BAD CONVERSATIONS

Most of us would be able to stomach bad conversations if they did produce some positive lasting impact. Bad conversations never truly end—they seem to linger in the form of certain negative outputs that can haunt relationships as well as organizations. In particular, negative outputs of a bad conversation fall under the following categories.

Bad Feelings

In bad conversations, there is a low level of listening and sharing of feelings, thoughts, and beliefs. The people in such a conversation can often feel hurt because of the lack of understanding or sharing. All of us take part in conversations that we regret. We make questionable commitments or poor decisions as the result of poor communication, lack of reason, or clouded judgment. And we feel lousy about it. This can indicate poor communication skills, hidden dialogue, or low levels of trust. High-Impact Leaders recognize such circumstances and actively check assumptions around sharing so these feelings won't result.

Bad Judgments

Bad judgments result from an incorrect or incomplete assessment of facts and conditions. Sometimes agendas are based on error. An agenda may have been created despite conflict between feelings and facts, poor reasoning and inquiry concerning assumptions and facts, or merely incorrect facts. High-Impact Leaders are careful to test assumptions, challenge facts, and uncover true feelings in order to increase the chances that they will address agendas properly. Many High-Impact Leaders rely with great success on gut feeling; either they are particularly perceptive and intuitive in the first place, or they are aware of their own limitations.

Sometimes errors are made in judgment because of the presence of undiscussables. When all facts or assumptions are not revealed, it is frequently because organizational levels of trust are low. Similarly, self-deception can happen when someone has a blind spot to an issue or fact. When levels of trust are low, honest communication is difficult. The innovators go unrewarded, and "yes men" and "yes women" abound.

Bad Decisions

Bad decisions take bad judgments a step further because they represent committed action. Bad decisions frequently lead to flawed programs, policies, and processes that are difficult to remedy. Once the products of a bad decision are in place, they are difficult to revise or remove, even in those organizations with high levels of trust. In organizations where trust levels are not high, bad decisions can linger for long periods because members of the organization feel powerless to change, make counterproposals, or question. Leadership effectiveness in such organizations is impeded because of the lack of confidence in the leader. This doubt is further exacerbated when a leader defends a bad decision despite a general recognition that the decision was misguided.

DECEPTIVE POWER

Sometimes leaders fool themselves: they believe that conversations are powerful or that trust is thriving, when this is simply not so.

I was called into a large manufacturing company to observe the leader's tremendous success with his senior team. The leader's aim was to showcase his team, document its attributes, and roll out its practices across the organization. He was eager to show off his accomplishments in this regard but told me in advance that he "didn't want to color my thinking or otherwise bias my observations by introducing the reasons for your visit to my team." He asked me to watch the open, rational, and expedited ways by which the team made decisions.

I observed the group work through a worldwide strategy for sales. The senior leader had prepared me to expect the best, yet what I saw was very different. Nonverbal and verbal signals alike indicated significant hidden dialogue, as the group seemed unwilling to say what was really going on. Canned presentations were applauded. Questions and objections were perfunctory and unchallenging. There was rapid agreement on assumptions, which were not challenged and seemed to override or leap past contradicting facts. There were some in the group who were eager, high energy, and open; their ideas (supportive of the leader's) went to the forefront. There were others in the group who were taciturn and restrained; their assumptions and statements were ignored and went unexpressed. The team quickly arrived at the sales strategy. True to the leader's predictions, the team had made decisions in an expedient fashion.

I could see why the senior leader believed that trust was alive in this group. The atmosphere of the room was very polite. It was collegial and friendly before, during, and after the discussion. Nobody expressed any negative words. Everybody supported the leader. Yet it was clear that this was not a great team coming to profound conclusions or moving decisively forward toward a great end.

As Peter Senge has observed, it is a myth that great groups are characterized by agreement and civility. In this case, I'm not suggesting that bickering and overwrought outbursts would have been indicative of a healthier team. The complete lack of argument suggested, however, that the group lacked trust, rapport, and a deep connection between the thoughts and feelings of the team members. I worried that this team, rather than standing out as an effective example of a group working through issues, was more a model of bad decision making processes.

Discussing my observations with the leader was painful. To his credit, after a certain period of protracted defensiveness, he was able to overcome his own hurt and wounded ego and see the valid indicators of the facts. Further observations of the organization at large led me to suspect that ineffective communication style was the cultural norm, the way the organization itself communicated. Although the leader was a career-long "company man," his eyes were nevertheless opened when I pointed out various other things I had observed. He saw suddenly that the emperor had no clothes. He could see why there were too many errors and too little innovation: the group was never really committed to action.

This leader ultimately deserves praise because of his openness to awareness and change. It is a difficult thing for any leader to change communication styles, especially when those styles are so ingrained in the culture around him or her. Yet this leader did change. When he confronted the group with this new information in a humble and deeply honest way, it turned into a powerful moment for both him and his group. When the group was exposed to the power of a truly connecting conversation that did not merely skip along the surface or give lip service to falsehood, there was a palpable sense of relief, as well as a refreshed and exhilarating aura of possibility. As a result, the group made its first long stride toward really coming together as a team with power.

This type of revelation is amazingly transformational. Conversations dictate results. Most times, truths, facts, and honesty are things that are stumbled around, sometimes stumbled onto, and, more often than not, ignored or avoided. There is a prevailing, unspoken feeling that truth and honesty sometimes bring pain. In my experience, the opposite is true. Bad conversations may bring a degree of short-term comfort in their avoidance of real, tough issues, but their long-term results are truly painful. They make us less than what we really are; they prevent us from achieving what we really can.

The responsibility of the High-Impact Leader is to rescue bad conversations and guide followers toward power.

THE SWAMP

Sometimes, despite our best efforts and most careful and rational interactions, conversations go nowhere. We become stuck in a bad conversation and there is seemingly no way out.

As I mentioned earlier, I call this place *the Swamp*. It lurks below the Tower of Power and is an area that is actually worth an occasional visit. I will explain why later. For now, let's focus on the chief implications of being stuck in the Swamp.

For Victims, the Swamp Is the House of Suffering

Some people are so hurt and damaged emotionally that they are unable to break free of those feelings. No matter what approach is taken or what overture is made, such people feel compelled to roll around in their own misery, sadness, bad experiences, past transgressions, and maligned positions. They refuse to see the opportunity to move forward toward constructive action that would rectify real or perceived wrongs. They either don't want to heal or aren't ready to heal.

You can heal sometimes by acknowledging wrongs. You can resolve buried conflicts by actively inquiring about emotions, sharing feelings, and taking emotional risks. The natural response to bitterness is to feel negatively toward that person. This response is often exactly what they want, but never need. By pointing out or openly acknowledging bitterness and hurt, you can make a victim aware of his or her behavior and the fact that such behavior is unproductive and unacceptable.

For Criticizers, the Swamp Is the Theater of Complaint

Complainers probably like to think they are only trying to improve things. I have even heard whining defined as "caring combined with powerlessness." When it comes to complaints about ideas, processes, or strategies, there is a difference between criticism and critique. Criticism is a negative approach that actively seeks to tear down and belittle, or to prove that something cannot be done, will not work, or does not work. Critique is another matter.

There is a time and a place for the rigor and in-depth questioning of critique. Sometimes, in the process of moving toward possibility and action, it is necessary to suspend an overly judgmental tendency, at least for a while. Most great ideas and innovations, not to mention deliberate work systems and practices, would not survive the slings and arrows of criticism in their early stages. It is through critique that ideas are given sea legs.

It is important to couch critique in factual observations, or to acknowledge such statements as observation. It is also important to be aware of how emotions are at stake and to state things in deliberately positive and supporting ways. You can overcome overcriticism in another person by actively pointing out that person's behavior and making clear that you will accept only more productive paths.

For Small-Minded People, the Swamp Is the Mud and Muck of Rumor

Some people choose not to support and foster the positive energy and culture of an organization. Rather, they actively spread hearsay, rumor, and innuendo. Often these types of people do this insidiously, behind the scenes, after the meetings, through e-mails, and on extended coffee breaks.

We all like to gossip about and analyze people, motives, happenings, situations, and events. However, some of us go too far and infect others with doubt, dispirit, lack of enthusiasm, and energy. It is important to nip such behavior in the bud, to point out that such a conversation is unacceptable or uninteresting, and to avoid fueling the fire by listening or upping the ante of observations.

For Passive People, the Swamp Is the Lounge of Resignation

Some people simply go with the flow. They are inactive about sharing emotions, information, wants, or needs. They do not want to test or challenge facts and assumptions, or make active commitments that bring about change. They are powerless, feel powerless, or choose to be powerless in ways that lead them to exhibit overtolerance, avoidance, and general "checking out." Such people may be misaligned with organizational goals. Alternatively, they may be poorly motivated, beaten down, lazy, uncaring, or unfit for the organization's environment. By seeking to uncover the roots of resignation, High-Impact Leaders seek to reenergize or realign (or else rid themselves of) a wasted resource.

THE SWAMP AS A SOURCE OF POWER

Sometimes, by acknowledging the Swamp, you can uncover important information. You can provide an outlet for pent-up frustrations, hurt, anger, and misalignment of personality and culture. People often feel a tremendous pressure to conform and align in ways that eventually sap energy, reduce enthusiasm, and establish bad habits and behaviors. The Swamp allows people to vent and uncover some tough things. Hundreds of companies, in fact, now use the term *Swamp Talk* as a way of referring to bad conversations. It seems to serve a need in describing this kind of behavior or incident, and in providing an impetus to refocus on the important issues.

One of the advantages of having the Tower of Power as a tool is that it objectifies the problems or issues in a conversation, removing them from association with a particular person or behavior. It is much easier to correct a bad conversation when you treat it in such a manner. Two people, growing heated in their discussion, can break the tension by saying, "Hey, look, we're in the Swamp now. Let's refocus."

The Swamp can also be used as a means to a productive end. A High-Impact Leader knows when the Swamp has been entered into and views that as a warning sign to be extra perceptive and inquiring. Sometimes, the Swamp reveals points of dissatisfactions or real problems. (See Chapter 9 on dissatisfiers as related to retention.) It may be a result of undiscussables, lowered trust, the mismatch of Say and Do, or poorly aligned systems, values, and stated goals.

Finally, the Swamp can also be a tremendous source of unleashed emotion. It is often difficult for rational people in a work environment to share sincere thoughts, personal feelings, and real wants and needs. And yet it is exactly such emotions that are the source of energy for reaching the power of a Powerful Conversation. By letting people descend into the Swamp, High-Impact Leaders can allow defenses to lower, feelings to emerge in unguarded ways, and people to fall back into their core patterns of behavior—their most basic wants and needs, the small seeds inside that form the outer shell. The Swamp is often the right place (albeit tangled, confusing, and dirty) to root around for a while in order to discover and uncover real values and issues.

GETTING OUT OF THE SWAMP

Still, a High-Impact Leader knows when it is time to reemerge from the Swamp. Too much time down there can be habit forming. Ultimately, a High-Impact Leader is focused on positive outputs, tangible results, forward direction, synergies of Say and Do, real channeling of forces, and real commitments. A High-Impact Leader views bad conversations as a nice place to visit once in a while for purposes of growth, breakthrough, and transformation—but not a place where people should live.

Keep in mind the following steps you can take to get out of the Swamp.

1. *Drop your agenda.* As soon as you hear Swamp Talk surface, recognize that you need to deal with it or the conversation will stall.

2. *Validate the issues and feelings.* It is equally important to dig in and uncover the roots of the feelings that drove the conversation into the Swamp (and that are keeping it there).

3. *Create a list.* One complaint or issue of resistance is usually the sign of more. Uncover them all and affirm and validate each one.

4. *Confirm the list.* Once you have a full list and the person agrees that nothing else stands in the way, review the list to gain clear understanding of the issues.

5. *Start with the last thing on the list.* Often, the first few objections are smoke screens, covering up other more difficult or deeply held convictions or problems. A bottoms-up approach usually brings faster resolution.

6. *Build up the issue.* Have the person tell you why the issue is so important to make sure you are dealing with all its dimensions.

7. *Hold up the mirror.* Establish the other person's line of reasoning and make it visible for examination. Often, doing so will expose a fallacy.

8. *Leave the Swamp behind.* Use the Tower of Power introduced in Chapter 2 to reframe the issue, unearth the assumptions, consider new possibilities, and craft actions that everyone can commit to in going forward.

POWERFUL CONVERSATIONS FOR BAD PURPOSES

There is another type of bad conversation that does not involve a descent into the Swamp. These are bad conversations masquerading as Powerful Conversations. These conversations are masterminded by people who intentionally employ the techniques and tools of Powerful Conversations for selfish reasons or as a strategy toward malevolent ends. These people are especially destructive because they represent a lethal combination of intelligence (in their mastery of Powerful Conversations) and ill motives.

These people are particularly difficult to spot, even for a highly perceptive leader, because they are highly intelligent, skillful, and careful at feigning the best intentions. Nevertheless, they use Powerful Conversations as a kind of poison, turning perception into misperception, trust into distrust. I call such people *Iagos* after William Shakespeare's character in *Othello*.

There is another type of person, commonplace in organizations, who cares only for his or her agenda and only pretends to listen, share, communicate, and engage. These people are actually interested in doing the minimum in terms of living commitments and arriving at shared goals and objectives. They really want only to maximize their own objectives, which usually comes at the expense of others around them. Such leaders are frequently strong, intelligent, and dominant, and are artful in getting what they want. They are able to feign authenticity, sincerity, honesty, and truth. Though they may achieve organizational goals and bring about short-term productive results, their actions and behaviors destroy organizational trust, a much more important long-term organizational asset.

Then there are those who are charismatic or particularly skilled in organization or manipulation. These leaders are the most destructive. Because of their positions of great authority or strong leadership, their actions and behaviors negatively impact a large number of people. Such a person is out of line with human values and principles, but is so strong and persuasive that values and perceptions become twisted. The Stalins and the Hitlers of the world were skilled at connecting deeply and fostering strong commitment and loyalty. We all know the power of their words—and the terrible consequences.

More often than not, however, bad conversations do not stem from malevolent people but are instead symptomatic of communication, personality, or organizational problems.

Bad conversations nevertheless represent an opportunity to turn toward power. By being conscious and conscientious of the Tower of Power as well as the symptoms and conditions of bad conversations, a High-Impact Leader can uncover the roots of problems and refocus and realign conversations on an upward path.

Conversations in the real world—the ones that take place amidst the pressures of getting work done, in the confusion of mixed signals, and with the clash of personalities—are difficult, slippery, and often unfocused events. Understanding how conversations function and how they achieve a movement toward results is the key to using them in skillful and artful ways toward positive ends. Such awareness reduces the occurrence of bad conversations and promotes the development of Powerful Conversations.

5

DIFFICULT CONVERSATIONS

COMMUNICATION IS NEVER easy. Inevitably, when a leader is driving change and dealing with conflicting agendas, some conversations provide a challenge that tests the bounds and skill of experience. During the heat of a difficult conversation, you need to fall back on a discipline. You need clear communication that advances agendas, promotes learning, and strengthens relationships. It's the difference between achieving objectives and having everything fall apart—and the difference between winning and losing.

Imagine having to let a close friend know that he or she is off a project because of poor performance, yet wanting at the same time to preserve the strength of the relationship. Imagine having to make necessary structural changes to an organization, realigning roles and positions in ways that involve cuts in the workforce, yet wanting at the same time to bolster morale and organizational commitment.

High-Impact Leaders routinely face such difficulties. They also need to exercise discipline that will enable them to forge positive outcomes from these kinds of situations. Powerful Conversations, through their structured nature and their focus on key, measurable outputs (advanced agendas, shared learning, and strengthened relationships), provide that kind of discipline.

Some people tell me that keeping the order and progression of a Powerful Conversation in mind when dealing with a routine issue is relatively easy. During a rational exchange, they say, it is easy to think back on the steps in order to move through "What's Up?" into "What's So?" and on toward possibilities and actions. But in dealing with messy real-life issues, they tell me, Powerful Conversations don't work. They simply wilt in the heat of a pressure cooker situation.

They're wrong. Powerful Conversations work best—and are indeed most valuable—when situations are the toughest and conversations the most difficult. In such trying times, adherence to the Powerful Conversation discipline can spell the difference between success and failure.

HOW HIGH-IMPACT LEADERS HANDLE DIFFICULT CONVERSATIONS

High-Impact Leaders are at their best during the hard conversations. They are able to muster the strength to confront and deal with what's not right. This does not mean that they are being confrontational, simply that they are not afraid to confront.

High-Impact Leaders can maintain such strength in the face of adversity because of their disciplined approach to communication. Leaders in general are not afraid of tough decisions. On the contrary, they welcome the responsibility. The reason in good measure why they are leaders in the first instance is because they are capable of contemplating hard facts and reacting decisively despite the strife, danger, or pain involved.

But some leaders cause tremendous damage in the wake of their decisions. As Daniel Goleman said during an interview conducted at Linkage's Global Institute for Leadership Development:

> Emotional Intelligence doesn't always mean being nice; it can mean being very direct, very assertive; it can mean making hard decisions; it might mean downsizing at some point. On the other hand, it means doing it with empathy, it means doing it intelligently. Often, tough CEOs have been brought in to squeeze the fat out. They end up so hated, and people end up so demoralized, that the CEO has to leave after the change is made. And that's because he or she didn't have Emotional Intelligence.

High-Impact Leaders have enough Emotional Intelligence to emerge from difficult conversations without being despised. But they do more than just survive such discussions. High-Impact Leaders manage to emerge from difficult conversations with relationships and trust at the very least intact—and often enhanced. They see a real opportunity for learning through such difficulty and stress—learning about themselves, about what moves them, about how they think, what they value, and who they are. They seek not only to learn themselves, but to get others to learn as well.

How can some leaders demote someone who has worked for them for a long time and still maintain (or even advance) their relationship with that person? It has much to do with empathy. It also has to do with caring and leading with the heart. Being honest with beliefs and feelings, as well as making clear and sincere expressions of personal agendas, help create the connection necessary for two people to discuss even the most difficult things.

The rules for succeeding in terms of having difficult Powerful Conversations include:

1.   Expressing compassionate feelings with sincerity
2.   Confronting fear with confidence
3.   Asking clearly what is wanted and needed
4.   Offering and commanding support, direction, and focus
5.   Making it crystal clear how everyone can win

All of this requires a grounded use of the technology of Powerful Conversations.

CONFLICTING AGENDAS

It is not uncommon for agendas to differ. This can naturally serve as the source of great conflict between people, halting learning and sinking relationships along the way. High-Impact Leaders make sure that they minimize the fallout from conflicting agendas by attempting to harmonize them. They know it is next to impossible to move their agendas forward without simultaneously moving forward the agendas of the other interested people. For commitment to be real, both parties need to know their efforts are in line with one another.

In a recent *New York Times Magazine* article, director Steven Spielberg discussed his production company, Dreamworks SKG, formed with former Disney vice president Jeffrey Katzenberg and music and film producer David Geffen. Spielberg is one of the toughest and most successful people in Hollywood. At the same time, he is undeniably sincere and trustworthy. The formation of Dreamworks shocked the movie industry because of the potential threat it posed. Indeed, it would have been seen as an open revolt against the big studio system if Spielberg hadn't lived up to all his various commitments with competing studios. He lived up to his commitments because of his values and despite the fact that this impeded the early progress of his own company. Nevertheless, doubts persisted about motivations. Asked outright whether he had joined with Katzenberg and Geffen because he wanted to help Katzenberg gain revenge against Disney, Spielberg dismissed the idea: "I didn't throw myself over the barbed wire so Jeffrey could have what *he* wanted . . . I threw myself over the barbed wire with Jeffrey and David so we could have what *we* wanted."

Such is the reality when agendas are shared or aligned (or at least alignable). Frequently, however, agendas are at cross-purposes and there is no easy way to reconcile them. Despite our best efforts, we cannot gain cooperation from the other person in achieving something that is important to us. In such cases, it is tempting to run roughshod over the wants and needs of that person.

I remember doing just that when I was at Raytheon in the Middle East during the mid-1970s. It may have happened 25 years ago and some 8000 miles away, yet the consequences still bother me to this day.

Like so many people early in their careers, when it came to negotiating with another person, I would sometimes confuse the concepts of push and pull. Instead of being direct, up-front, and honest in order to win people over (i.e., pulling them in), I thought that the power and the winning came from pushing. I was willing to flex the force of my leadership by pushing my agenda over and through people's opinions, beliefs, and feelings. I saw uncovering wants and needs as largely irrelevant. Where someone stood in my way, the easiest and most leaderlike solution was to knock that person down.

Now, years later, I recognize that this is a short-sighted approach. The best thing that can be said about flexing your muscles is that it might lead to a fleeting, short-term victory. This type of strategy, however, gives no thought to promoting learning or strengthening a relationship. No real power comes from it. And no one can truly achieve any sort of long-term agenda or build a lasting coalition without the support of others.

My ambition in this particular case was to create a leadership development program for a division of Raytheon. It was high profile and had the backing of the company's president. From my point of view, the program was terrific, incorporating the best leadership development practices from the best companies worldwide. I met with the senior team to give my presentation and thought I had agreement in the room from everyone. I was wrong. There were a number of people who indicated through their actions that they did not support me.

I was convinced that one person in particular was not going to support the effort. I felt that Tom was just not straight with me about his opposition to our plan. He avoided key meetings, stalled on decisions, and, in a number of small ways, created impediments to the program's success. In any conversation we did have regarding the program, he said the right things. When it came to delivering on promises that I thought he had made, though, he was always missing in action.

I boiled on this for a long time. I finally decided I was going to confront Tom with the issue. I was convinced direct and open conversation was the answer. I knew about *hidden dialogue,* the conversation going on below the surface where real thoughts and needs are played out. I had to drive out and expose Tom's hidden dialogue. I wanted to hear it from him. I wanted him to say that he was not with me, that he had intentionally failed to live up to his surface support.

I had a meeting with Tom the next day on another matter and I used that opportunity to address his seeming nonsupport of the program. "Tom," I said, "I have a bone to pick with you. I don't think you're behind me on my leadership development program. In every situation where it seems there is an opportunity to make this program a capstone for the entire organization, I'm not sure you're there. It almost seems that you are trying not to help me, when you promised to do so at the meeting. A commitment is a commitment. You are going to live up to it, aren't you?"

Tom listened to me as if I were coming from another planet. This angered me further and I repeated my demand. "I know you're doing this. I want you to admit it and tell me now whether you're going to back me from here on." Significantly, I didn't ask him about his agenda, how he was feeling, or what he needed.

Tom was shocked and became angry. He told me I had no right to say what I was saying. He wasn't going to change because I didn't like the way he performed or acted. I argued with him on it further. He clammed up. We parted angrily.

I had my chance to push my agenda the next day and made a great mistake. The president of the company called me and asked how the program was proceeding. I told him things were moving along. He asked if there was anything holding us back. I knew this was a free ticket to make it clear that Tom was not carrying his weight. I knew I was taking a risk, that I was crossing a line, but I thought I had no choice. The success of the program demanded it and, what's more, I had offered Tom the opportunity to come clean with me and he hadn't.

"There's one issue I could use some help on," I said. I wanted to soften it and not sound like I was betraying Tom. I just wanted to put enough pressure on him to get what I wanted and needed. "I'm not getting all that I need from Tom and I'm a little worried that his heart isn't in it 100 percent."

The president asked me how I could be sure about Tom's lack of commitment. I explained that Tom was not saying anything negative directly, but that in subtle ways he was being unsupportive.

The words still bite into me 25 years later. I felt justified in exposing Tom to the president because I had talked with him directly the previous day. It wasn't like I was going behind his back. Nevertheless, I sensed immediately that I had done something very wrong.

The president said he would take care of it. I never heard another word. Tom appeared noticeably more supportive but he didn't talk with me on a personal level for the remainder of my employment with the company. Even at social gatherings when we were in the same room with a small number of people, he made it clear that he wanted nothing to do with me.

The lessons of my "victory" were all that was left. I had won a useless fight. I never uncovered—and still don't know to this day—the roots of Tom's resistance, or his agenda, wants, or needs. It was a Powerful Conversation that never happened.

Today, older and wiser as they say, I recognize that my real loss was Tom's friendship. I had great memories of early days with him, but now all that was gone because we never had the necessary Powerful Conversation. Even from a business standpoint, my tactics had been poorly conceived. I had lost an ally, and lost the chance to win over someone whose contributions could have made my program last. I had certainly lost the opportunity to get Tom's support the next time I needed it. His trust in me was nonexistent. I broke one of the cardinal rules of trust by failing to show him I cared for him; instead, it was all about my agenda.

After that incident with Tom, I was smart enough to shelve those tactics for good. Unfortunately, some leaders spend their entire lives embroiled in a succession of such incidents with people who, for some reason, refuse to support the leaders' agendas. I see the effects of clashing agendas all the time. It is a particularly sad thing in family relationships. I am frequently consulted by leaders of thriving organizations who are deeply troubled by relationships with their own children. We talk about how Powerful Conversations can work there, too—how expressing emotions, determining wants and needs, and making commitments in a deliberate fashion can lead to the strengthening of the relationship. Clashing agendas need not (and should not) hamper something as important as the relationship with your child.

SEPARATING WANT AND NEED

When agendas clearly don't match, spending time in conversation uncovering what is really causing resistance is critical. Nail down the facts. Find out whether there are any alternatives to getting done what one side or the other wants to do. See if there is any flexibility to the agendas. There usually is.

Classic negotiations for a business deal or contract are characterized at their outset by conflicting agendas. The best negotiators are very adept at patiently letting the entire story come out before they determine what the real dealbreakers are. In other words, they find a way to separate *want* and *need.*

Up to now, I have used these terms in tandem, but their subtle differences are important to note with respect to difficult conversations. In principle, wants are more easily sacrificed than needs. Needs are closer to the bone. They are where we are more vulnerable. We often mask wants behind needs in an almost defensive way, even insisting that our wants *are* our needs until the end. During negotiations with labor unions, management may hear many wants. It is the ability to translate and understand what the union really needs that mitigates disputes. In any conflict, if all parties were satisfied only by getting everything they wanted, agreement would hardly ever be possible. For the most part, agreement arises when needs are finally uncovered and settled on.

When the difficult conversation involves two talented people, negotiating through wants and needs can also be the path to success. Take basketball superstar Michael Jordan, who recently retired with a closetful of individual awards, six championships, and unreserved adoration. It is almost impossible to remember that, in the late 1980s and early 1990s, he was considered by some to be a loser. His unbelievable individual talent brought him scoring titles and MVPs, but his team (the Chicago Bulls) always came up short in the playoffs. Ultimately, Jordan's leadership ability—and Jordan himself—were questioned. Many held out Larry Bird and Magic Johnson as the real winners, the guys who delivered in the big games, got the most out of their teammates, and won NBA titles. Jordan's accomplishments paled in comparison.

Then, in the early 1990s, Phil Jackson came on board as the coach of the Chicago Bulls. Many wondered how long Jackson would last and whether he would be able to "handle" Jordan. Jackson did—through the use of a Powerful Conversation. In particular, Jackson sat Jordan down and told him he had decided to install a new "triangle offense" that would give Jordan's teammates more shots. Jordan, by contrast, would get fewer shots. His scoring would likely go down and he would have to sacrifice some of his individual statistics. He might even lose his firm grip on the NBA scoring title.

Jackson knew that this alone would bother Jordan tremendously. He wanted to make sure Jordan knew from the outset how tough the transition would be. He wanted no surprises so that Jordan could commit to the system completely should he choose to do so, fully cognizant of the difficulties. He told Jordan that sometimes he would see teammates like John Paxson, Scottie Pippen, and Bill Cartwright miss shots Jordan could make in his sleep. It would be frustrating, but it would get everyone on the team involved. It would promote leadership from all quarters, something that would be needed in the playoffs at the end of close games—something that was necessary if Jordan and the Bulls were to win a championship. Specifically, Jackson told Jordan:

> This is what you've got to remember. Maybe these guys are not as talented as you'd like them to be, but this is as good as they're going to be. And this is as good as we can get under the present situation. But if we run a system, everyone is going to have an opportunity to perform. They can't do the spectacular one-on-one things that you can do, but they can have some level of success and perform on some level, even in critical situations. . . . Teams just don't win with one man doing all the scoring, because when you need to you can shut down one individual, and Detroit has done that to us. . . . We need to score as a group, and score consistently as a group, to win.

Still, Jordan was reluctant. The new offense threatened his most closely held wants (scoring titles, etc.). Jackson's skill as a leader was in asking what Jordan *really* wanted—in other words, what he needed. That answer was easy: what Jordan needed, both to quench his competitive spirit and to cement his reputation, was to win a championship. Without a championship, his status as a great player would be tarnished despite his unmatchable play as an individual.

So, eventually, Jordan agreed to subsume individual statistics to an offensive system that he doubted but that offered the allure of what he needed: an NBA championship. That spring, the Bulls won the first of their six NBA titles of the 1990s. In the final series, Jordan, of course, was the main man, but unlike past years, this time he received plenty of help from his friends. Phil Jackson had been right. And, because of that Powerful Conversation, Michael Jordan had finally become a champion.

MATCHING INQUIRY AND ADVOCACY

Skillful inquiry is the key to unearthing hidden dialogue and finding the white space between wants and needs. When you are frustrated, surprised, or puzzled by a person's lack of support for your agenda, it is sometimes necessary to explain your point of view more clearly. When you want to explain your point of view, do the following:

1.   State your inference.
2.   Provide your data.
3.   Explain your reasoning.
4.   Ask for reactions.

It is usually more effective—and always more difficult—to dig deeper into the other person's point of view. When you want to understand another person's point of view, try these tactics:

1.   Restate what you heard (the person's inference).
2.   Ask for the person's observable data.
3.   Ask for the person's reasoning.

Taking these steps in reasonable, rational, and objective ways can lead to a more open and sharing discussion. Sometimes, it comes down to a matter of making people aware of their own intransigence by exposing them gently to the facts.

This can all be very difficult for people from upbringings characterized by poor communication styles. We are all products of our *primary learning*—those patterns of behavior, belief, and attitude we learn in our earliest days as children. For the most part, when we grow older, most of us are able to function in ways that depart from our primary learning in social or work situations, as the circumstances may dictate. Confronted with a difficult situation, however, fear and uncertainty prevail. At such times, we are quick to return to primary learning patterns. The discipline of Powerful Conversations can help pull us back.

AGREEING TO MOVE ON

Leaders are always pushing their agendas. They can be guilty of pushing too hard, however. For example, if one of our leaders at Linkage did not want to go into a new business area and I absolutely wanted us to, I would have to spend time uncovering his or her assumptions about this. If I were to demand that he or she proceed without respect for his or her resistance, my victory would be short-lived because the other person's commitment would not be heartfelt. Digging in, I might find that his or her resistance is due in part to other factors—a lack of expertise or interest, for instance, or an overloaded plate of existing responsibilities. Together, we could probably come to solutions that alleviate the problem, supplement the lack of resources, or otherwise help us both out. It is a fundamental truth that you cannot push your agenda past someone else. High-Impact Leaders are always taking other people's agendas into consideration and integrating them into their own.

Returning to the example with the reluctant leader: in the final analysis, if my agenda were still too strong and the other person's cooperation too weak, I might have a Powerful Conversation with him or her about my need to move forward without his or her support. Sometimes, differences cannot be resolved. In such cases, an amicable separation becomes the real goal of a Powerful Conversation. In being honest and clear about my needs and how they differ from those of the other person, I would nevertheless try to maintain our relationship. I would then try to find someone else who would step up to the plate and deliver. There are times when a leader must say, "I know where you are on this, but I have to get it done. I need to go forward and do it without you. You understand my position. Let's commit to not having this be a wound or grudge between us."

Sometimes, unfortunately, a High-Impact Leader has to move on, even if it results in a grudge or negative fallout. Consider, for example, Harry Truman's handling of the Douglas MacArthur situation during the Korean War. Truman's clear agenda was to keep the war a limited one in order to minimize the loss of American lives. He didn't want to tangle with China or the Soviet Union, but strove instead to ensure that it remained a short-term police action. And Truman clearly tried to enlist MacArthur in that agenda. He even flew to Wake Island to meet with the general in the hopes of winning him over.

Truman, of course, was the commander in chief, and MacArthur—a good soldier—dutifully obeyed his orders, at least for a while. But the general clearly had grander designs for the war. He made a number of moves independent of the White House that Truman ignored in the hope that MacArthur would come around. But MacArthur never did. And, when MacArthur issued an inflammatory declaration to the Chinese threatening to expand the war at the very moment Truman and his staff were preparing a cease fire proposal, Truman knew it was time to move on. Still, the president didn't act hastily, remaining steady and exploring all the possibilities and implications. He knew firing MacArthur would be a political disaster. MacArthur was, arguably, the most popular man in America in the early 1950s. But Truman had an agenda—one that he strongly believed in, and one that was fundamentally and irretrievably inconsistent with MacArthur's own agenda. So Truman fired MacArthur.

The fallout was predictable. The president was lambasted in the press and hung in effigy throughout the country. The general, on the other hand, was hailed as a hero and greeted with a ticker tape parade in Manhattan. Through it all, Truman remained steadfast and confident. He had known he would take a short-term hit, but he also knew his dismissal of MacArthur was best for the country. Eventually, the criticism of Truman (and the love affair with MacArthur) subsided. Truman was vindicated after all. It was his conviction in his agenda, and his wisdom in knowing when to move on when MacArthur (despite Truman's best efforts) proved to be antithetical to that agenda, that were the key to Truman's triumph.

PREPARING FOR A DIFFICULT CONVERSATION

Just as a lawyer prepares for court, or a musician rehearses before a performance, it is critical that a leader prepare for a difficult conversation. Walking into a difficult conversation without adequate preparation can feel like approaching a hornet's nest without protection. The importance of being prepared is illustrated by the contrasting stories set forth in the following paragraphs, each of which involved the firing of a high-level executive.

In the first case, the chairman of the board fired the president of his organization but failed to make the discussion associated with the firing a powerful one. The chairman had consulted with me in advance concerning the rules for a Powerful Conversation. We had planned out how it would take place and what would be said. Nevertheless, the chairman's discomfort with such a difficult situation led him to falter in his execution of the steps of a Powerful Conversation. He failed in the clarity of his message.

It was almost comic in its tragedy. I visited the president after his meeting with the chairman to debrief and coach. From the beginning, I was confused. The president was distressed and somber but was not devastated. I initiated a discussion about how his interview with the chairman had gone.

"Well," the president said, "we had a conversation. He said he was upset about some things. He's not going to allow this to continue. I think I'm in a lot of trouble."

"How much trouble are you in?" I asked.

"I really have to find some solutions for this. If I'm not careful, I have a feeling I'm not going to keep my job."

Believing that the conversation had been intended as a termination, I was obviously surprised. I dug into what the chairman had said and what the president had heard. It even turned out that they had come to commitments, supposedly clear, at the end of the conversation. According to the president, the chairman's instructions were to "take the weekend to think about what we talked about."

"I need to put a plan together to correct things," the president told me. "He was very clear when he said that we cannot go on like this."

I had to tell the president, in as difficult a business conversation as I have ever had, that in fact he had misinterpreted the chairman's words. He had already been fired. It was not the way he deserved to be let go. It was an unfortunate and tragic way to find out and I did my best to minimize the damage. It was necessary, although painful, that I be absolutely clear in the Powerful Conversation that we then had.

As difficult as it is to give bad news, it is equally difficult to hear it. Part of the heightened need for clarity is due to this difficulty in receiving the message. When someone hears bad news, it can be so devastating that he or she focuses on only one aspect or a narrow aspect of the information. When someone is told, for instance, that he or she has cancer, he or she often cannot possibly hear—and does not hear—any message about options involved with treatment. Sometimes it is necessary to have a difficult conversation in stages, holding back one part of the bad news until the initial impact has truly sunk in.

Scripting can also help. During difficult discussions people can leave things out. High-Impact Leaders know this and prepare. Difficult conversations have a parallel with how the best lawyers prepare for cross-examination of a witness. They sketch out the situation in advance. They know what they will say; they know what will be said in return; and they prepare for any variations in that exchange. While they have a final objective in mind, they have as many of the tangled sidebar outcomes as possible mapped out and prepared for. High-Impact Leaders prepare in such a manner for their difficult conversations. And, at the end of those conversations, they double-check to make sure the person actually heard the right message, as scripted out.

In the other firing situation I would like to relay, a script was used. Because of this preparation, the result was more effective and successful for all involved.

The president of a large subsidiary of a Fortune 50 company had made a decision that his COO was no longer a viable person for that position. The COO had fallen completely out of favor with the board. His style was somewhat abrasive and confrontational and, when he took a couple of missteps, the board jumped on him internally.

The president knew the firing of the COO would be tremendously difficult on both a personal and professional basis. The two had worked together a long time. A change initiative in the middle of organization-wide implementation had been the brainchild of the COO. The change effort might collapse if people in the organization felt that the COO had been treated unfairly. To make matters worse, the COO was an emotional person. The president knew he would receive the news badly. It was possible the COO would be angry enough to try to create as much havoc as possible on his way out.

The president asked me to help him prepare. He wanted the decision to have minimum organizational impact, if possible. He wanted the COO to receive the news with dignity and to go out gracefully, if possible. And he wanted their relationship to remain strong so that they could continue to work together functionally in the interim while the search for a new COO took place.

We used the Tower of Power. We rehearsed. The president wrote notes and practiced. He prepared his clarifying questions in advance. He worded how he would announce the news. We rehearsed the things not to say. He could not say, "I feel as bad as you." It would be a trigger because the bad news was really about the COO. He could say, "I know this is hard. You are an important person to me and I want to find a way to help you through this. The impact of this can be tough on us." We practiced the body language.

I was supposed to join them 20 minutes after the president broke the news. When I neared the office, I could see them through the glass talking. I could actually see the expressions on their faces. They were leaning close together. They were deeply engrossed. I saw the shock and disconcertment on the COO's face become a more softened and accepting grimness. I could tell, even though the schedule had called for me to join them then, that they were deep in their discussion concerning the greater meaning of this incident and that they were working through important issues related to their relationship. I knew that they could use the extra time.

When I returned an hour later, I joined them to discuss next steps. They were ready for me then, having fully connected with each other in the most difficult of circumstances. The tone of the discussion and their willingness to work together on this made it clear that their relationship would survive.

OVERCOMING ADVERSITY

Then there are times when situations are so bleak that the conversations must achieve an intensity, a gravity, and a sincerity necessary for people to make life-changing decisions together.

On the July 4th weekend of the summer of 1991, things took a sudden and very devastating turn in the young life of Linkage, Inc. In assessing where to go next, our COO, my brother, and I met in a discussion that we still call "Three Men and a Couch."

We had just lost a major piece of business with our prime client and we were in complete shock. We didn't have much of a backlog to speak of. And most of our employees had elected to remain behind with our former client. In one day, we had gone from a thriving start-up of 30 employees with a large office and a multimillion-dollar client to—literally—three men and a couch.

I personally was devastated. It was not only the loss of what I had built with so much blood and sweat. I felt worse for having let down our group. In point of fact, I had failed them completely. My guilt weighed on me with a terrible, pressing force. I could see only the error of my ways.

I had made a strategic error of mammoth proportions. It was the kind of mistake you read about in introductory level case studies at business school. You do not rely on only one source of revenue. In my arrogance, I had ignored conventional wisdom. I had thought the rules were not written for me, that I could handle a tricky situation, walking a tightrope that others wouldn't risk. I had let us put all our eggs in one basket, and now we were paying the price. In my hubris, I had brought others down with me, people who relied on me and who had believed and trusted in me.

My brother, Jim, was one matter. We were family and we had been through tough times before. I knew our bond of trust and commitment was solid no matter what happened. I felt worse with respect to the third man on the couch, Larry. Just months before, this longtime friend had joined me in a gesture of support.

We had worked together years before at Raytheon. As our careers progressed, we remained friends, meeting for lunch or dinner in Boston's North End. He had shared in my vision for Linkage (helping me sketch out goals and the rudiments of a business plan on the backs of cocktail napkins), but couldn't join initially because he had only recently accepted a position with another firm and wanted to honor his commitment to that company. Two years later, he had finally been free to join us, knowing full well that we were young, entrepreneurial, and somewhat of a risk compared to a stable, large organization. Larry was 43 years old with two small children. He needed the security of an income. But suddenly, on the morning of July 4, we were clientless and without prospects. I was devastated at how I had let him down.

It was one of those conversations no one knows truly how to handle. It came from the gut. I spoke directly with Larry and Jim in a way none of us will ever forget. I told them how badly I felt. I couldn't reasonably expect them to continue with me. If I were Larry, having rolled the dice and lost, I knew I would say, "Phil, it was fun, but it didn't work out, so I'm going back to Raytheon for the security of my family." I knew there was absolutely no way I could convince Larry to overcome any doubts now and continue on with our enterprise. The only person who could convince Larry was Larry, and there was nothing for me to offer except my support.

I told Larry and Jim that I still had the vision to go on with this business. I was already able to see our next steps. The potential was so clear to me—right before our eyes. But that was me. I couldn't expect Larry and Jim to see it that way.

I offered my support no matter what they chose to do. If they decided to continue with me, I would support them financially for as long as I could with steady salaries while we rebuilt the business. In my mind, we had the opportunity to build a world-class company. I was of the opinion that sometimes your hard luck can be your good luck. I had seen what John Keane had done. I knew we could do it, too.

On the other hand, if they decided we should part ways, I told them I would split the remaining equity among us, and they would have some level of financial support to compensate for the lost earnings while they pursued alternative employment. If they decided to leave and I was still able to pull off what I thought we could do, I promised they could return to the company whenever they wanted. Even years later, if the company had grown beyond what we could imagine on that day sitting on the couch, they could come back, without hard feelings, with no regrets or questions.

We talked about it, weary but rational and even hopeful about our options. Still, I knew we needed time. We needed to connect with spouses and families and tend to our wounds and shock. We needed to come to agreement with our loved ones around future paths.

Larry later told me that the message had been powerful—that he had found it impossible to turn his back on someone who had demonstrated so much loyalty and confidence. We still shared the same vision. We still had the same key people who could implement that vision. On Tuesday after the long weekend, we were making sales calls for our new venture.

It really was a defining moment for Linkage. No one welcomes that type of heartache. Yet out of that heartache grew the greatest business achievement of our careers—building a world-class company from scratch and against all odds. A few days after that Powerful Conversation on the couch, the first of several other key employees came over to join us, drawn to our vision and values and lured by the opportunity. Those people are still with us, the core of our company today.

This time, we made sure we diversified the business. The new vision included streams of product and service lines organized around a few core competencies. We knew it would succeed. And we worked hard to make it happen.

One of our adversaries later confided to me that we had gotten lucky in parting with our former client when we did. Internal problems there emerged soon after, and a serious erosion in the revenues of the institution resulted. We, on the other hand, had come up with a new business model and an equity position to boot. In the end, it was a good move for us.

And it supplied a lesson I never forgot: even in the worst of times, and amidst the most difficult of situations, a conversation can drive us forward toward great ends.

POWERFUL CONVERSATIONS IN PRACTICE

POWERFUL CONVERSATIONS AND TRUST

I HAVE LONG thought of trust as a critical ingredient for bringing people together to do work. It was only when I closely examined the importance of communication as it relates to leadership—and how High-Impact Leaders communicate through Powerful Conversations—that I truly came to see how trust functions, why it is important, and what it does for the organizations and individuals involved.

The outputs of a Powerful Conversation are an advanced agenda, shared learning, and a strengthened relationship. In combination, these outputs lead to a deepening of trust. Successful leaders purposefully use Powerful Conversations to create and build trust in their immediate relationships and, by extension, within their organizations at large. Why do they bother? Do they get some sort of personal satisfaction out of knowing that people trust them? Or are they simply engaged in an altruistic attempt to build a more humane or pleasant work environment? Not at all. Rather, High-Impact Leaders build trust because it is an asset they can leverage and deploy as a competitive advantage to create bottom-line results. High-Impact Leaders recognize that trust enhances their capability to achieve goals consistently and sustainably.

In this chapter, I want to discuss what trust is and how it works. We will examine how High-Impact Leaders view the importance of trust, and how they themselves foster trust within their organizations. I will show you step by step how trust is built and how it varies in effect, depending upon its depth or level. I will also analyze how trust is lost—because trust is the most tenuous of assets, and without clarity, consistency, and intent, it quickly depreciates. I will relate all of this back to the central subject of this book—Powerful Conversations.

THE ESSENCE OF TRUST

We begin our analysis about the nature of trust with a brief story about Herb Kelleher, CEO of Southwest Airlines, as captured in Robert K. Cooper and Ayman Sawaf's book, *Executive EQ:*

> One day, Gary Barron, executive vice-president at Southwest, caught Kelleher in a hallway after a Front Line Forum, the regular meetings in which Kelleher gets together with senior employees to focus on how to improve the company. Barron told Kelleher he wanted to talk about the complete reorganization of the management structure of Southwest's $700 million maintenance department. He handed Kelleher a three-page summary of the plan. The CEO read it on the spot, and raised only one concern. Barron said that it was something he was concerned about too, and was dealing with it. "Then it's fine by me," replied Kelleher. "Go ahead." The entire conversation took about four minutes. Kelleher is trusted. He has credibility with his employees.

This story illustrates what many of us think about trust: we don't know exactly what it is, but we recognize it when we see it.

Trust is the currency of leadership. It is rooted in the very essence of why people follow other people. While trust may be easy to recognize from a personal and emotional standpoint, it is more difficult to define in any concrete or quantifiable way. Certainly, trust is most frequently thought of as a by-product of a relationship rather than as a goal in itself.

I submit, however, that the inverse of the preceding statement is true: trust should be the goal of a relationship and not merely a by-product. Trust, after all, produces the conditions that move relationships forward toward productive goals and results. Trust is not just nice to have or a mere expression of positive feeling, but a necessary condition for sustained high performance and impact. Keep in mind that humans are emotional animals who release their strongest commitments and contribute their best abilities only under certain conditions. It is trust that is the key to the source of the most powerful emotions upon which leaders can rely to guide and influence the actions, thoughts, feelings, objectives, and even dreams of others.

But what is trust as an emotion? Even its definition is nebulous. It connotes a belief in the integrity and character of another person and an ability to rely on that person in a predictable and consistent way. Trust allows you to put aside doubt and misgivings and let yourself succumb to the vision, ideas, actions, or suggestions of another. This feeling ranges widely in circumstance, but perhaps not so widely in psychological content. I think, on the one hand, of a child being told by a parent that he or she will be caught at the bottom of the slide; and, on the other hand, of an audience of worldwide employees listening to a CEO explain the benefits of a new venture requiring everyone's commitment and strongest efforts. Both circumstances require a feeling of trust to believe that the suggested action will lead to the promised results.

Where does trust live? Where does it manifest itself? As a feeling, trust is most frequently experienced between individuals, on a one-to-one basis. Trust also lives in the relationship between a leader and a group of followers. Finally, trust is a critical element inside groups, existing between group members interstitially, like an ether or fluid.

In each of these instances—between individuals, between a leader and a group, and within a group—the existence of trust pays enormous dividends. When trust exists in individual relationships, there is ease in communication. Less effort is required to make decisions, take actions, or move forward to a common goal. When a leader is trusted by a group, his or her words have credibility. Strategies and goals—even ambitious ones—more readily gain buy-in and support. Finally, when trust exists within groups, a sense of energy and common purpose prevails. There is nothing within reason that a group of people who trust each other cannot accomplish together.

On the other hand, lack of trust between individuals, between a leader and a group, or within a group spells immediate and long-term trouble. When trust is low, doubt and suspicion rule. It is difficult to move forward toward common understanding and focused action. It is, for that matter, difficult to accomplish anything of substance.

As I stated earlier, I aim to turn your thoughts about trust upside down. While we naturally think of trust as a nice feeling fostered by the achieving of goals or the furthering of a relationship, we should really think of trust as a necessary means to a goal and a well-trodden path to deeper relationships. It's not a "chicken or egg" debate: trust leads to goals and deeper relationships, not the other way around. In addition, whereas we define trust by emotions such as certainty and faith, I want to analyze the emotions that trust produces—trust's outputs, so to speak—namely loyalty, confidence, calmness, intimacy, hope, and commitment. Given that trust has these outputs, and that those outputs can be measured, perhaps trust is not as "soft" as you initially might have thought.

Finally, I want to become more concrete about the way we define trust. In particular, I believe we should look at specific levels of trust. Although we can easily say that "we trust so and so a lot (or a little)," the actual gradations—the markings of the levels—are harder to pinpoint. This chapter focuses on defining those levels as they apply between individuals, between a leader and a group, or within a group.

After we have looked at how trust operates and how it is valued by High-Impact Leaders, I think you will agree that all of this is critical. I hold that the building of trust is possible because trust, rather than being just a feeling or a condition or a by-product, is truly an act of will.

EXPEDITED DECISION MAKING AND RAPPORT

Let's think again about the story Cooper and Sawaf told about Southwest Airlines. Given a three-page brief, Herb Kelleher was able, in just four minutes, to okay a $700 million decision presented to him by his executive vice president. Cooper sees the level of trust employees had in Kelleher as the lesson of this engagement. I am equally impressed by the level of trust and confidence Kelleher had in his VP. In any event, it is a wonderful example of the power trust has to expedite decision making and enable people and an organization to move forward toward meaningful goals and objectives. In other organizations, where trust isn't quite as pervasive, that decision would have taken months or years—or would have been made too late or not at all.

Rapport was the reason the decision was made so quickly and so well at Southwest. Rapport comes into being when you engage in Powerful Conversations in a relationship already infused with trust. When you have a connection that is strong, you can move quickly beyond the barriers that initially stall most conversations. Think of a person with whom you have genuine, deep, and honest rapport—a person you can really talk to about almost anything. I am fairly certain this rapport grew out of moments in which you and that person connected deeply through meaningful conversations centered around vulnerability and shared hopes.

I thought about the importance of rapport recently when I attended the bar mitzvah of a friend's son. At the ceremony, the story of the Tower of Babel was told. Before the Tower of Babel, all humankind spoke only a single common language and could communicate and work together with ease. When the tower was being built, however, God took away that ability. The resulting confusion made it impossible for the builders to work together, which is why the world's peoples are scattered and we have so many languages. In reality, of course, the plurality of languages in this world is a wonderful expression of the variety of cultures that exists. Still, for anyone who has contemplated the difficulties of communicating with others or the immense gap that sometimes must be overcome to make a complete connection with a fellow human being, this story cannot help but ring true.

Observing the bar mitzvah that night, I was struck by the specialness and staying power of the ceremony. This is a ritual that has traveled over many centuries and vast geographical distances. I listened closely to what was said—the promises, the expressions of honesty, the statements of how the boy felt, and his openness about what he wanted and needed in his life. Suddenly, I realized that, in its ritualistic way, this ceremony was a Powerful Conversation!

My serendipity went even further. In this particular ceremony, the rabbi focused on exactly the issues at the heart of a Powerful Conversation. He said, "There are so many feelings in our lives that need to be expressed that it is important to say clearly what you need and want." And then he said something I will never forget: "The rainbow has two sides. On each side is a promise, a covenant, a commitment. In order for people to understand one another and to make these commitments, they have to be able to take the chance to say what they feel, need, and want." The rabbi might as well have been describing the way in which Powerful Conversations build the rapport and the connection between two people.

In business, I have seen the very best High-Impact Leaders do exactly that with each other. When the rainbow connects completely, High-Impact Leaders develop rapport. They display an ability to communicate in half words, glances, and nods. When trust has broken down barriers, High-Impact Leaders enjoy the highest forms of Powerful Conversations.

It is through rapport that decisions are made quickly and agendas advanced fluidly. This can happen, of course, between individuals or within a group. The Kennedy brothers are one famous example. Isaiah Berlin described the interaction between Robert and John Kennedy in this way:

> The rapport between the brothers was absolutely astonishing. Whenever either spoke to the other, the understanding was complete, they agreed with each other, they smiled at each other, they laughed at each other's jokes, and they behaved as if nobody else was present. One suddenly felt there was this absolutely unique rapport, such as is very uncommon, even among relations. They hardly had to speak to each other. They understood each other from a half word. There was a kind of constant, almost telepathic, contact between them.

I have seen High-Impact Leaders develop this type of rapport with other leaders or entire groups. I have studied it and I know its foundation is trust. It is the trust that comes about in the wake of a string of Powerful Conversations and fulfilled commitments. With this type of trust, there are no undiscussables, no vulnerabilities. When trust reaches its highest levels, connections are complete. Conversations are expedited rather than complicated by nonverbal signals. Body language, looks, and reactions are all signals that provide the reassurances for moving forward with understanding and action. It is an amazing thing to behold.

TRUST AS ORGANIZATIONAL ASSET

High-Impact Leaders value trust as a tool for achieving organizational goals and as an asset with unlimited rates of return. In fact, trust is the only asset they possess that they can deploy for impact on a consistent basis in a wide variety of contexts. Trust is the only tool a leader can consistently use as a medium for interactions with individuals and groups, in close proximity or at global reach.

Imagine for a moment that you could lead only through traditional means—namely influence, request, and authority. Now examine the gap between those means of leading and the actions and feelings that are considered so necessary to realize the goals of leadership—committed action, loyalty, tremendous striving for common goals, unstoppable momentum. Can a leader create all this through influence, request, and authority? Of course not. High-Impact Leaders consciously cultivate trust because they recognize that it provides them and their organization with an energy to achieve great ends.

But don't just take my word for it. At Linkage's 1997 Global Institute for Leadership Development, a panel of distinguished CEOs met to discuss "Lessons of Leadership." Moderated by Warren Bennis, this panel included Bob Haas, chairman of the board and CEO of Levi Strauss & Co.; Max DePree, chairman emeritus of Herman Miller; and Bob Galvin, chairman of the executive committee of Motorola. When asked which fundamental truth of management had remained unaltered by the coming and going of countless fads and theories over the years, the panel immediately focused on one thing: trust. Their insights around creating a trusting and intimate work environment were both profound and inspiring. Allow me to quote from their discussion, as later recounted in *Training & Development:*

> *Bennis:* With all the changes you've seen and expect to see, what one fundamental truth of management still applies?
>
> *Galvin:* Integrity hasn't changed as being a supreme requirement. And I consider trust to be the greatest motivator.
>
> *DePree:* I agree with Bob on the matters of integrity and trust. I would add that trust takes a lot of moxie and commitment to build. It takes a long time, and you can lose it overnight.

Haas: I think there are two essential things. The first is the value of people, and the second is the importance of values. None of our enterprises are worth anything—Motorola's great technology, Herman Miller's brilliant design, Levi's innovation and heritage—without our people. People are what make it happen. So, as a leader, I focus on enabling and encouraging people.

DePree: We're becoming more interdependent. The way that you focus on people is by learning how to establish and nurture relationships. Technology is wonderful, but it's not sufficient. Relationships are the things that enable technology and all our other skills.

Bennis: How do you build trust in large institutions?

Haas: I don't think there *is* such a thing as a large institution. I think there are organizations that *behave* like large organizations. Our work experience is as intimate as our work groups. Leaders create an environment that is intimate and defines how an individual feels about the larger enterprise. We [Levi Strauss] have 36,000 people in over 60 countries around the world. That's a huge, sprawling enterprise. There are pockets of it that feel enormously personal and exciting, and where bonds of trust and mutual commitment are characteristic. There are other parts that are grinding, dull, impersonal, and horrible, and I think all of us recognize that picture in most of our enterprises. Our goals as leaders are to amplify the intimacy of every work group.

These leaders of large, global, and successful organizations deem trust—not market share or new technology or cost effectiveness—to be the most important asset a leader can possess and nourish. They see trust as the seeding ground from which other critical outcomes grow. As that panel observed, trust is difficult to build and easy to lose. It is also intrinsically connected to the values of the organization as well as the principles of commitment and enablement—something we have previously explored in Chapter 3 in our discussion of the trust-building type of Powerful Conversation.

THE FOUR C'S OF TRUST

Leadership is an awesome responsibility. It is a complicated and demanding task to achieve goals as a leader—far more difficult and complex than achieving goals as an individual. If raw intelligence and hard work were all it took, High-Impact Leaders would abound. But leadership involves more than that. A leader must not only be able to invoke the collective abilities and emotions of others, but must also raise these things up to their highest levels. It is often said that leaders shouldn't try to do it on their own. They can't. They need to utilize the power of trust to get others to move in the same direction with them.

Building trust, then, is a central goal of leadership. Only with trust will others freely offer their support and best efforts. It is therefore important to understand the various dimensions of trust. As Max DePree observed in the panel discussion mentioned earlier:

> To build trust, the first step is to respect everybody. One way is to understand that it's not an intellectual commitment; it's a matter of the heart. The second way is to discipline yourself to take everybody seriously. Another step is to keep your promises. A leader who's confused about who she is will lead a group who's confused about who they are. So, it's impossible to have an organization in which trust is a meaningful element if leaders don't keep their promises.

I would boil down the essence of DePree's observation into the Four C's of trust: *caring, commitment, clarity,* and *consistency.* Figure 6-1 demonstrates these elements and their interrelated nature. Together, they go a long way in defining trust.

Caring

When Max DePree talks about "respecting" and "taking everybody seriously," he is referring to the importance of caring. Caring is hard to do—

FIGURE 6-1   The four C's of trust.

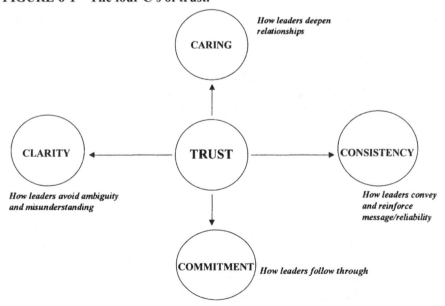

and I don't say this flippantly. It is, as DePree suggests, a discipline. It appears to be a particularly difficult challenge in a large organization. As Haas observed, however, there is no such entity as the large organization— only smaller groups and individuals that make up the overall organization. This brings caring down to a more intimate and possible level.

Each of us has only limited time and emotional energy. Fortunately, the dimension of caring has a domino character and effect, as one act is invariably multiplied many times over within an organization. Specifically, an act of caring inspires other acts of caring; a story about caring ripples throughout the organization to become part of the collective understanding of who the leader is and what the organization stands for in terms of values. My former boss at Raytheon was a leader who knew the value of caring. Jim Lewis would go out of his way to make sure you knew that you were the most important person he was dealing with at the time. In every Powerful Conversation in which he engaged, he tried to demonstrate caring through what he said and did. He later told me that this was his investment in trust—an investment that never ceased to pay dividends. And, of course, he legitimately cared. If he hadn't, if it had all been a calculating front, his trust-building effort would have backfired, and whatever trust he had previously established would have quickly eroded.

Commitment

DePree's reference to the importance of keeping promises also captures a fundamental tenet of trust. Trust is a fluctuating commodity that rises and falls in perceived value, depending on the state of the operative relationship (between individuals, between a leader and a group, or within a group). This value is measured by how much believability we ascribe to another's promises or commitments. If somebody says he or she will or can do something, does he or she then make that commitment come to life? High-Impact Leaders ensure that all of the commitments to individuals and groups they make during Powerful Conversations come to life. And with good reason: leaders are fundamentally and mercilessly judged on the relationship between what they say and what they do.

I think we have all had experiences involving this, either as leaders or as those who follow (and judge) leaders. Think of the speech that President Clinton gave after his acquittal on impeachment charges in February 1999. Whatever your feelings about Clinton's culpability or sense of accountability, he was clearly conscious of the trust that he had jeopardized. He apologized specifically for what he "said and did" that had broken the faith. He knew he had not kept his commitment to the American people.

Clarity

The existence of clarity is also a critical success factor in building trust. During Powerful Conversations, a leader cannot be vague about his or her commitments or messages. Beyond surface unambiguity, a leader must also be acutely aware of how a given message is being received and interpreted by its recipients. Without such disciplined efforts, misunderstanding is a strong possibility. I have seen intelligent and rational adults on both sides of a misunderstanding assert and really believe that they had agreed to two entirely different things stemming from the same conversation.

This common phenomenon reminds me of the game children play when they whisper something person by person around a circle so that they can laugh at the garbled message that results in the end. Such a result is no laughing matter in the business world, with millions of dollars on the line. High-Impact Leaders know they cannot afford to be unclear in their communications if they hope to cultivate trust.

Consistency

Finally, trust involves and hinges upon consistency. Indeed, trust is a living thing requiring repeated demonstrations to maintain. Arbitrary statements or acts, or even arbitrary outbursts, can lower or destroy trust. It is the constant reinforcement and reestablishment of messages, goals, and rewards over the span of a series of Powerful Conversations that helps build an environment of trust.

High-Impact Leaders find no shame in repetition. They repeat a message or a vision or a story or an attitude like a mantra, like a chorus in a song, until it takes hold and comes to life in the actions of others. Mark Tolosky of Baystate Health System in Western Massachusetts is such a leader. I have seen him repeat the same leadership theme over and over again—in a variety of contexts and over a long span of time. Eventually, however, Tolosky's theme echoes in the phrases and terms of his employees. This indicates that the people have taken his message to heart.

Other leaders, however, overlook the importance of consistency. They are not totally in sync with respect to what they say and what they do. For example, a leader may give a great speech about diversity or gender equality or the importance of teamwork, but then undermine the effectiveness of that speech by telling an off-color joke or participating in an unfair assessment of someone. It is amazing how quickly the story of the leader's inconsistency will spread through the ranks. This inconsistency, of course, depletes trust in the leader. High-Impact Leaders would never model such a disconnect. They painstakingly attempt to achieve consistency in their messages.

THE RULES OF TRUST

The Four C's flesh out the various dimensions of trust, but they don't really answer all the hard questions. Why is it so difficult to build trust? And why is trust so easy to lose?

The answer lies in human nature. It is not a natural inclination for human beings to trust. They are, by nature, suspicious of those they don't know. Trust is also a function of an individual's own psychological ability to trust. For example, a person who has been raised in a nontrusting environment or a situation of abuse will find it very difficult to trust. Backgrounds aside, a new situation always involves zero-level trust. When you first join a new team, you trust neither the team nor your new teammates. Nor do they trust you. You are dealing with your own issues, perspectives, wants, and needs, while the rest of the group needs time before it can begin to trust you.

High-Impact Leaders consciously try to create trust, and there are tools they use to build it. We've talked about Powerful Conversations as a vehicle for building trust, and the Four C's as the dimensions of trust. Now let's see if we can reduce this to a series of statements that come closer to explaining why trust is so hard to gain and easy to lose. I call the following series of simple but powerful truths the *rules of trust.*

1. *All trust begins with a commitment.* This is the first rule of trust. High-Impact Leaders lay the foundation of trust with commitments. They grow the trust by keeping those commitments.

2. *Trust requires being clear and consistent.* High-Impact Leaders scrupulously ensure that their commitments are understood and reinforced. Clarity and consistency establish the proper channel for communicating the specific commitments the leaders plan to keep.

3. *Loyalty can only be obtained through consistent acts of caring.* Once High-Impact Leaders demonstrate that they consistently keep their commitments, a sense of loyalty is possible. High-Impact Leaders use caring to foster that loyalty. They demonstrate a series of acts of caring to build loyalty around them. This caring must be genuine if loyalty is to arise. Disingenuous caring can, in fact, create disloyalty.

4. *Trust requires living one's own beliefs.* High-Impact Leaders engender trust around them by "walking their talk," i.e., taking actions that are directly in line with their stated beliefs. Conversely, failure to live one's own beliefs destroys trust. If, for example, a leader is caught in a lie or in an act that is in direct opposition to his or her

professed belief, trust that has been built up over time through kept commitments and acts of caring will disappear—overnight.

5. *Total trust involves an interlocking system of internal beliefs.* Belief systems "seal the deal" in the building and sustaining of trust. If belief systems are shared between and among individuals, total trust is possible. High-Impact Leaders intuitively know this. They therefore seek to build trust with individuals who have belief systems compatible with their own, and actively search for opportunities to integrate these separate but compatible belief systems into one shared set of beliefs.

By understanding the rules of trust and the ways in which the variables meet and complement each other, we can take more deliberate steps toward building trust. Powerful Conversations are the best vehicle for doing so— they are the method by which you can make clear and consistent commitments, express acts of caring, act in accordance with your professed beliefs, and explore opportunities for forging shared beliefs. Now let's examine the levels of trust so that we can truly understand what we are trying to build.

THE LEVELS OF TRUST

The notion that trust has levels is easy to understand. We even have common expressions that indicate levels of trust. We say, "I trust him or her to an extent," or "I trust him or her completely," or "I'd follow him or her anywhere." More specifically, I think of trust as having three levels (see Figure 6-2). Each

FIGURE 6-2   The levels of trust.

level has its own measurements, behaviors, and outcomes. And each level is a connected step below or above the next level.

Through their actions and behaviors, individuals and organizations can move up or down the levels. Organizations that cannot even get to the first level of trust are in trouble. When trust is nonexistent, undiscussables abound, teamwork is hampered, information flows poorly, confidence and loyalty are low, and efforts are misdirected.

For the most part, real-life organizations are a hodgepodge of trust levels. Some leaders manage to function effectively and steer organizations adequately with only certain rudiments of trust. Leading organizations to greatness, however, requires bringing trust to a much higher level. In fact, I have never seen or read of a case in which a leader has obtained greatness for his or her organization without first obtaining and fostering high levels of trust. High-Impact Leaders consciously seek to bring their organizations to those heights.

Level One Trust

Level One trust is about commitment. I call this type of trust *professional trust.* It is the most basic and important level to obtain in order for an organization or a relationship to be highly productive. Within Level One trust, the commitments that flow up, down, and across the organization are cut and dried, with very little gray. And these commitments are, by and large, kept. Unfortunately, few organizations or relationships operate completely under the principles of professional trust—probably because few organizations recognize the vital link between simple commitments and the power of trust.

Commitment itself is an act of will. To be conscious of commitments requires, as Max DePree suggests, discipline as well as clarity. The equation is simple. The act of keeping a commitment builds trust; the act of breaking a commitment reduces trust. In an organization in which keeping commitments is a priority, employees accept and have faith in the relationship between Say and Do. This provides for a tremendous clarity in processing information, making decisions, and taking action steps.

Organizations that enjoy professional trust are functional, rational, and enjoyable places to work. Employees and systems are in sync. Productivity and effectiveness are natural by-products. All in all, an organization with Level One trust is not a bad place to be.

Level Two Trust

With Level Two trust, even greater things happen. Level Two trust is defined by the loyalty that can stem from the kept commitments that take place with Level One trust. When coupled with caring, these commitments can blossom into a loyalty that is deeper and more reflective of people's feelings for one another. The fact that caring is the key gives Level Two trust a personal dimension and is the reason I refer to this level of trust as *personal trust*. You should note that the climb in levels here is cumulative; personal trust presumes that an organization or a relationship already lives up to the commitments of professional trust (which is no small assumption).

Organizations with Level Two trust become more than good places to work. They are, instead, homes for people who really care about one another—and homes for those willing and eager to devote their best efforts for a long period of time.

Level Three Trust

Level Three trust connotes the highest level of trust, something I call *total trust*. Level Three trust is an even loftier state than the previous levels because Level Three trust is about belief—specifically, the ability and willingness to demonstrate and live a shared set of beliefs. To trust someone at this level means that you have the same kinds of values, goals, and perspectives. Level Three trust can arise only after Level One and Level Two trust are in place. I therefore use the following equation to define the condition of Level Three trust: ***total trust equals commitments plus loyalty plus shared beliefs.***

In organizations or relationships that enjoy total trust, great things are possible and, indeed, frequently happen. Think of any "great group" and you can perceive a common, shared set of beliefs that emerged despite a wild diversity of personalities. Consider the team inside Apple that developed the Macintosh computer, for example. That group, out of a deeply felt and shared need to "make a dent in the universe," overcame all odds to design a new level of computer. Despite Steve Jobs' many infamous dysfunctionalities as a leader, he was able to create total trust and thereby bring his group together and direct it toward a groundbreaking end. There are other famous examples, of course: for one, the scientists at the Manhattan Project who developed a weapon they thought would improve the chances for peace and the preservation of democracy; for another, the group of men and women led by Nelson Mandela who developed democracy after apartheid ended in South Africa. With total trust and the belief that is at its heart, there is no limit to what a group of people can accomplish.

THE HOWARD SCHULTZ STORY: DEMONSTRATING COMMITMENT, CARING, AND BELIEF

As another concrete example that demonstrates trust in action, consider the story of Howard Schultz. As the president and CEO of Starbucks Coffee

Company, Schultz has emerged in recent years as one of the top entrepreneurs of the twentieth century. He has taken a simple community-oriented idea to create a "third place" between work and home and developed that into a powerhouse global concept centered around coffeehouses. Perhaps most importantly, while building this mega-corporation, he has done something that puts him in a special category. Schultz is the type of leader who builds great loyalty within his organization (and to himself) through what he says and does. He is a tremendous example of a person who delivers on commitments and demonstrates caring in a way that backs up his powerful words. In short, Howard Schultz drips of trust.

Schultz's upbringing in Brooklyn was modest. Through the community of families, shops, and services in the neighborhood, he developed a fundamental belief in the fairness and dignity of employees. When Schultz was still a boy, his father became unemployed. Because of that, his family ended up without benefits. Schultz never forgot the indignity of this for his family, nor the destruction of morale, self-esteem, and security that stemmed from being in a family without access to health care and other benefits. This experience helped forge Schultz's strongly held belief that benefits for all employees are a critical ingredient of today's moral company.

When he founded Starbucks, Schultz lived up to these values by changing the established covenant of benefits to a new model based on loyalty and caring. Howard Schultz makes sure every employee is well taken care of—even if he or she is not a 40-hour-per-week, long-term employee. In the early years of Starbucks, Schultz made these commitments by communicating directly with store managers, employees, and his management team around the United States. Schultz also backed up his words with action. He never defaulted on his promises and cemented his reputation by delivering on his commitments time and time again. In other words, he established Level One trust between himself and his workers through his living commitments.

A terrible event in the mid-1990s, however, led to an expression of caring that deepened the trust between Schultz and his employees even further. During the robbery of a Starbucks coffee shop in Texas, the store manager was brutally murdered. Howard Schultz responded to this tragedy with what to others would seem uncustomary urgency—and in a way that vividly illustrates how a High-Impact Leader secures a higher level of trust. Schultz immediately chartered a plane to Texas. After closing the store, he stayed on site for days, meeting with employees and family members, providing counsel and support, and demonstrating caring at the deepest and most sincere levels. But he didn't stop there. He established a fund for the family of the slain manager. He dedicated the store to the manager's memory. And he devoted the store's profits to supporting the manager's family and the education of his children.

Think again about what Schultz did. He stopped everything he was doing and flew to Texas—not the next day or a week later, but that night. He met, cared for, and counseled employees and their families. And he continued to ensure that this caring was felt at a higher level, giving up profitability and dedicating the store to the slain manager. What he was doing— simply and powerfully—was living his beliefs. He had talked about these beliefs and used them in speeches and small acts that established a certain amount of trust in him as a leader. Now he was reinforcing his words with a genuine act of caring.

I know (and he himself would be the first to admit) that Howard Schultz is no angel. He is a tough and strong competitor with ambitious goals for worldwide market share. But in studying the particular success of Starbucks, I have been struck by its flexibility, decision-making speed, and sense of community, despite the decentralized nature of its franchise business. These strengths clearly stem from things like strategy, focus, drive, innovation, and systematized work processes. I also believe that they are a product of trust.

Without trust and without Schultz's living vision of a corporation with traditional neighborhood store values, I do not believe Starbucks would have succeeded to the extent that it has.

HOW TRUST BREAKS DOWN

Trust is a slippery slope. Think of the acknowledgment by Max DePree that "trust takes a lot of moxie and commitment to build. It takes a long time, *and you can lose it overnight.*"

For the most part, trust falls apart inadvertently. It's tempting to think bad actors within the organization somehow sabotage trust, but that is rarely the case. In fact, breakdowns in trust are usually a by-product of lack of clarity and lack of discipline. What so frequently happens is that misunderstandings and bad feelings develop in the gray area between Say and Do, in the undefinable middle ground of ambiguity. This gray area is fertile ground for misinterpretations; it is the place where expectations, commitments, and actions misalign.

Trust can erode as well because of unrealistic standards. Many of us approach trust in the following way, expressed by a vice president of a company that once engaged me as a consultant: "I give everyone a 100 percent benefit of the doubt and start docking points when they let me down." The vice president had the math all wrong—it's not a matter of series of subtractions, but of addition. To start off by trusting a person and then scaling down by docking points is to miss the main thrust of building trust. It's not about docking from 100 down to 0; it's about building from 0 to 100. Trust naturally develops in a slow buildup over time through openness and living commitments. Powerful Conversations help accelerate the development of trust, with an accompanying structural buildup of understanding and rapport.

Other proven trustbreakers to keep in mind include what Dan Goleman describes as an "amygdala hijack"—an instantaneous emotional reaction or outburst in response to a situation. Erratic emotional outbursts are a sign of low Emotional Intelligence and a proven trust breaker. Disingenuousness, as I have mentioned, may fool some of the people some of the time, but is certain to be spotted by those with high levels of perception. And talking behind someone's back (or otherwise exhibiting behavior that indicates that what you say in one situation differs from what you say in another) is also a sure way to reduce trust.

Finally, you should be aware that trust fluctuates—and that what you perceive as a breakdown may just be a mere fluctuation. There is, for example, a constant process of gaining and losing trust going on within organizations, groups, and families. This process reflects the complex mix of expressions of wants and needs, commitments and beliefs, and action and inaction that affect the overall atmosphere of trust. So often when I am asked to analyze a leadership team, I am told there are enormous problems involved. Frequently, these problems are because of fluctuations in trust. That is why it is even more important to have Powerful Conversations that clearly record facts, action steps, and commitments.

REBUILDING TRUST

You can assess the damage of lost trust through something I call the Avenue of Pain (see Figure 6-3). The diagram clearly maps the actions that break trust and the personal feelings that arise as a result. The further down the Avenue of Pain one goes, the more difficult it is to regain or build trust.

Rebuilding trust is a long and sometimes painful process. Again, Powerful Conversations help. Powerful Conversations that aim to rebuild trust start with an acknowledgment of the damage and the resulting pain. A new set of wants, needs, and commitments usually arises from the ashes of this damage and pain. Clearly establishing these is a step in the right direction.

It is also helpful to spend time together in the Swamp, allowing the hurt person to vent his or her feelings about the broken trust and transgressions. Rebuilding trust ultimately requires a renewal of connection. And there is no better place to foster such a renewal than in the Swamp. By engaging in

FIGURE 6-3   The avenue of pain.

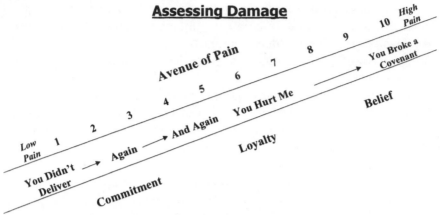

Swamp Talk and reconnecting around wants and needs, you can initiate the process of letting go. Forgiveness can then begin to take place.

Finally, it often becomes possible to redefine the rules around commitments during this rebuilding phase. When trust has been destroyed, there will naturally be strong doubt as to the viability of any future commitments. Addressing this fear head-on is the best way to ensure that such commitments will be honored. For a relationship plagued by a breach of trust, it is essential to acknowledge the wrongdoing and begin the process of rebuilding the elements of professional trust. Rebuilding trust (just like building trust in the first place) starts with the commitments that are the bedrock of the Powerful Conversation.

7

THE AGENDA
FOR CHANGE

POWERFUL **C**ONVERSATIONS **ARE** fundamentally instruments of change: they compel change through the learning they foster and the action steps they demand. In the hands of High-Impact Leaders, Powerful Conversations are the most effective tool available to communicate, ingrain, and ensure the success of organization-wide change.

Driving productive change is the real work of leaders. For a senior leader faced with the mammoth task of steering an organization through change, there is a profound need to be strategic, efficient, and directed in his or her messages and interactions. When faced with such challenges, High-Impact Leaders use Powerful Conversations intentionally, deliberately, and in line with an overall change strategy. All of this strikes at the heart of what the best leaders do and how the best organizations win.

In this chapter, we will look at how a High-Impact Leader can formulate a vision of change and effectively communicate it to the right people in the organization. I call this vision and process the *Agenda for Change.* In the next chapter, we will look at how High-Impact Leaders use missionaries of change called *Passionate Champions* to infuse the Agenda for Change throughout the organization with dramatic, sweeping, and cascading effect. When the vision of the leader carried forth by Passionate Champions becomes part of how the employees think, talk, and act, the Agenda for Change is complete.

COMMUNICATION LINES AND WORK FLOW

The complexity of any organization is numbing to contemplate. Imagine, for a moment, the diversity of people and the variety of their duties and day-to-day tasks. Think of function heads, vice presidents, and project managers involved in marketing, finance, operations, and research and development. Consider the ways in which all of their efforts, roles, and responsibilities intermingle in producing the outputs of the organization. Even if you manage to chart out how work is supposed to flow and function, drawing clear lines that connect various squares and triangles, you would fail to accurately reflect the messy ways in which organizations really operate. Any attempt at tracing real work flow would end up in a blur of scribbled lines.

What is most amazing to me, on top of all this, is that no two organizations are alike. Organizations, like nations or tribes, exhibit their own traits and customs and have their own unique practices, beliefs, and accepted modes of behavior—in short, their own cultures. When you take an individual out of one organization and place him or her in another, more often than not that person adjusts by taking on the habits, expressions, and perhaps even the ways of thinking of the new surroundings.

Now imagine that, as leader, you are faced with the need to implement deep and lasting organizational transformation. You seek the aid of structured chains of command and channels of communication, knowing that there is, in reality, much more to the way the organization actually operates and communicates. In fact, from a mile above, you see very little real communication traveling along the proper channels. Instead, you hear a buzz of noise from the talk going on inside, outside, and around the connecting lines, reflected in a blur of e-mails, memos, and meetings. The lines are all tangled. And, at the end of the day, you cannot be sure the right message is getting across to the right people.

High-Impact Leaders influence culture, direct work outputs, and drive change at levels unmatched by others. They do so through their targeted use of Powerful Conversations. To understand how, let's first look at the nature of an organization's culture and the role conversation plays in producing change.

CONVERSATIONS AND ORGANIZATIONAL CULTURE

There is an emerging school of thought that supports the theory that an organization's culture is created by the intertwined and multiple series of conversations taking place within it. In working with numerous senior leadership teams, I myself have observed how experienced and mature individuals with distinct personalities nevertheless share a common language and communication style in their interactions. I would take it a step further: among leaders of the successful organization, there is a dramatically increased chance that assumptions and perspectives are also shared in common. This isn't just an interesting footnote. It is critical, for I also believe that common language is the first step toward common action.

Jeffrey D. Ford and Laurie W. Ford made tremendous headway in our understanding of this phenomenon with their 1995 article, "The Role of Conversations in Producing Intentional Change in Organizations." Along with that of other significant researchers, the Fords' evidence suggests that all verbal speaking is performative, i.e., it is made up of speech acts that are a combination of action and language. These verbal acts bring into existence a social reality that did not exist before their utterance. In other words, culture derives from conversations, and change itself is linguistically based and driven. It follows that intentional change is produced by intentional communication.

One of the central themes of this book is that the structured and intentional nature of conversations permits High-Impact Leaders to use them in targeted ways to drive results that are ultimately about producing change. I call such events Powerful Conversations, and I believe their impact on organizations is profound. Trust is created by the alignment of words with actions and the advancement of relationships. This raised level of trust produces, in turn, a higher base from which further Powerful Conversations (and more change) can proceed faster and more effectively. The net result: more effective communication, higher levels of trust, and an enhanced capability for change.

Deliberate, transformational, and lasting organizational change is made more possible and more likely by using Powerful Conversations in intentional, strategic ways. High-Impact Leaders employ such conversations within a formal Agenda for Change process to drive such results.

THE AGENDA FOR CHANGE
The Agenda for Change is a deliberate, structured approach to transformation. It supplies the framework that brings strategy from the level of "vision" and "mission" to the reality of common language and committed action. Unfortunately, many organizations and their leaders succeed in articulating a vision or a mission, but only a precious few manage to take the next crucial step. The Agenda for Change—the pathway for that transformation—is achieved by mapping out a communication strategy that pinpoints the loci and stages where change needs to occur. With the map in place, change can then take place through a series of Powerful Conversations.

The Agenda for Change reflects a view of the organization that largely ignores hierarchy in order to effect real transformation. In the Agenda for Change, the leader does not stand at the apex of a pyramid of command, but acts as a free and roaming radical able to engage in Powerful Conversations where they are needed most in order to influence the organization at its most receptive and productive points. High-Impact Leaders who develop an Agenda for Change use Powerful Conversation technology deliberately in order to positively impact short-term and long-term business results. They are, in effect, able to steer an organization from vision and strategy to the operational level of execution. And Powerful Conversations are the vehicle that takes them there.

Like others who work in organizational effectiveness, I have more often than not seen attempts at deliberate change frustrated and turned back. Deliberate change is such a difficult, shifting, sliding, unwieldy, and unpredictable endeavor. With the Agenda for Change, however, I have seen impressive results take hold in expedited and efficient ways. Over the past few years, I have been fortunate enough to help several different leaders institute their own agendas for change. Let me tell you about how one of those transformations was conceived, planned, and implemented during a five-year journey.

THE STORY OF ONE LEADER AND AN AGENDA FOR CHANGE: JEFF OTTEN AND BRIGHAM AND WOMEN'S HOSPITAL

It was 1994, and Boston-based Brigham and Women's Hospital (BWH), one of the world's best academic medical institutions, needed to change. BWH's president, Jeff Otten, saw clearly that in order for BWH to continue to be successful in the long run, it could not glide along on the momentum of its current accomplishments; the world of health care and medical technology was changing far too quickly for any such passive approach.

Jeff recognized that the complacency engendered by BWH's tremendous success would serve as an additional blocker of change. He therefore made a concerted, purposeful effort to understand how change is implemented in an organization, how culture is sustained and fostered during change, and how leaders and managers most effectively envision, communicate, and implement change. I was fortunate enough to join him in a formulation and step-by-step implementation of his resulting Agenda for Change. Along the way, we learned much about the effective use of Powerful Conversations and the role of trust in creating what Harvard Business School professor Rosabeth Moss Kanter has called a "change-adept organization."

Let me say from the outset that, through our journey, I learned more from Jeff Otten about Powerful Conversations than he did from me—despite the fact that I introduced the concept of Powerful Conversations to Jeff. Like all great leaders, Jeff recognized the value of this technology instantly and saw its importance to his embryonic Agenda for Change. On top of this, Jeff has management skills that match his tremendous leadership skills. He is incredibly able in actually executing the strategic initiatives to support his vision; after all, a plan without strong implementation is worthless. Jeff Otten is one of those High-Impact Leaders who combines the virtues of a visionary with the operational skills of someone who understands how work actually takes place.

In 1994, Jeff Otten's need was to develop an operating platform for a strategy that was clear. BWH needed enhanced learning agility so it could remain a leader in advanced medical practices and technology. It also needed the financial discipline required to maximize value in a ruthlessly competitive health care marketplace. Jeff recognized that these twin goals had to be in seamless accordance with the mission and values of the institution if they were to be embraced by the doctors, nurses, medical staff, and financial managers who care so much about health advancements that they devote their lives passionately to the cause.

On a personal level, Jeff knew he would have to broadcast his message continually and consistently in order to reinforce the principles of the movement. He knew he would have to show the organization how to live its beliefs through a series of Powerful Conversations.

THE ROLE OF THE LEADER IN THE AGENDA FOR CHANGE

Today, Jeff Otten insists that his role as leader was insignificant in the success of his Agenda for Change. He proclaims the virtues of the people throughout the organization and calls them the real heroes because they are the ones who actually did the work that made the initiative a success. What Jeff is being modest about, however, is his multifarious role as activator and enabler of those people.

Let me use Jeff as an example to show the qualities High-Impact Leaders display in obtaining results inside and throughout institutions during their Agenda for Change.

1.   *They listen to and spend time with employees at all levels of the organization.* Time and again, I observed Jeff putting on a hospital gown and walking the floors to talk with patients, doctors, nurses, medical assistants, staff personnel, kitchen personnel, and anyone

else connected to BWH. He approached people, in other words, at the level where real work is done; he did not overly focus on the administrative or financial sectors of the hospital, where the work is merely processed.

2.   *They are caring people who are very direct.* I learned from Jeff that caring does not mean being circumspect or touchy-feely. Jeff tells it like it is, in the language that is most conducive to getting the message across. Throughout implementation of the Agenda for Change, he was very clear about what he wanted and needed from people and he was equally clear about his own commitments.

3.   *They do exactly what they say they will do.* Jeff is another leader I have noticed who carefully writes down his commitments and is sure to follow up. Throughout the change initiative, people throughout the organization knew that when he made a promise, he would deliver.

4.   *They do not let the strategy overwhelm the people.* Despite having an overall Agenda for Change in mind, Jeff did not confuse people with the multiple aspects of the strategy. Rather, he pulled people into the strategy, focused them according to their jobs, and complimented them for their accomplishments.

5.   *They are incredibly open to diversity.* Jeff is open to divergent opinions and perspectives with due respect. During his Agenda for Change, he was not only willing to entertain opposing views, but also altered his decisions and actions in light of the input when appropriate.

There is a common thread running through these five factors: willingness and ability to learn. Like all High-Impact Leaders, Jeff Otten is a person who is always learning. He seems on a constant search for new information and data. He is also extremely knowledgeable and aware of the various constituent groups in his organization. Like a sociologist, he is observant of groups and behavior. He builds relationships with key members of each constituent group to show that he cares and is eager to get each group what it needs to succeed.

THE STEPS IN AN AGENDA FOR CHANGE

Now that we have captured the essence of Jeff Otten's leadership, let's examine how he drove his Agenda for Change. Here are the five specific steps that he took—and that you can follow to drive your own Agenda for Change:

Step One: Develop the Agenda for Change vision by setting the goal and clearly defining the objectives. Your specific objectives might involve meeting a certain cost savings target or reaching an enhanced standard of quality. Regardless of the particulars, make sure your goals are clear, tangible, and defined in an achievable way.

Step Two: Focus the senior leadership team on defining and fine-tuning the architecture for the Agenda for Change. At a macro level, what sort of task forces, committees, meetings, special projects, initiatives, and the like are needed to actualize the vision? To operationalize his vision, Jeff formed a senior leadership team to build the architecture of the change process. The senior leadership of your organization needs to craft a master blueprint to make sure the structures are in place to effectuate the change and achieve your objectives.

Step Three: Focus managers at all levels on the vision and objectives. At the micro level, how will the change be carried out? Jeff engaged the commitment of managers throughout the organization to oversee the implementation of that vision. In this step, the managers who direct the daily action in the trenches are the key. Senior leadership needs to translate that vision and those objectives to managers in the form of specific action steps. You can employ Powerful Conversations to do so.

Step Four: Institute a learning system. Every change effort with which I have been involved requires learning—and unlearning—if it is to be successful. Jeff realized his Agenda for Change, by necessity, had to focus on the core competencies driving the technological aspects of the business. To this end, he realized his Agenda for Change would need a learning system that would cultivate learning around these competencies. Make sure your Agenda for Change focuses on your organization's core competencies as well. In that way, you will ensure that the entire organization is learning the critically important information that differentiates you in the marketplace.

Step Five: Ensure that Passionate Champions are heading up specific, critical components of implementation and operation. Even with the right vision, architecture, action steps, and learning, an Agenda for Change will flounder if the right people are not connected passionately to its vision. To this end, make sure you enlist

Passionate Champions (discussed more fully in the next chapter) in your cause. These people are the missionaries of change. Because they are convinced of its necessity, they make it happen up, down, and across the organization—or, equally importantly, in their little (yet critical) corners of the organization. The Passionate Champions at BWH included nurses and leaders in business unit clinics, in academic medical centers, and in advanced practices like cardiac surgery. You will need to identify and enlist the Passionate Champions in your organization who will carry out your Agenda for Change.

So, Jeff defined the success of his Agenda for Change around three groups: (1) senior leaders who could build the architecture, (2) highly skilled managers who could tie the Agenda for Change to business systems and processes, and (3) Passionate Champions who could drive the change. There is a natural interplay among these three groups. Jeff Otten brought his strategy to life through exactly that interplay.

He also used Powerful Conversations with members of each of these groups to ensure that they were playing their part. Powerful Conversations were, in fact, the critical success factor for each of these groups. Senior leaders came together to support the Agenda for Change through Powerful Conversations. Managers executed the Agenda for Change by using Powerful Conversations at all levels inside the institution to spread a prescriptive energy originating from the vision. Finally, Passionate Champions became encouraged, motivated, and energized to make their part happen in the most effective way and at the highest levels through Powerful Conversations.

ACHIEVABILITY, BELIEVABILITY, AND TRANSFERABILITY

Jeff and I have defined a three-step process that we call *achievability, believability,* and *transferability.* I am convinced that this is a remarkably apt description of how a change strategy is defined, disseminated, and implemented with effectiveness.

Once a change initiative is envisioned, the High-Impact Leader works with his or her leadership team to determine how it can come into being. Doing so provides the Agenda for Change with *achievability.* A key point here is to define real outputs that are concrete and achievable, not vague goals that cannot be quantified. One way to end with concrete outputs is to form a vision of where the organization wants to be and then work backward to define the necessary steps required to make the vision happen. Such a process is essential to crafting a coherent message about the Agenda for Change.

By enlisting the support and commitment of key figures throughout the organization, a leader secures *believability* for his or her Agenda for Change. Powerful Conversations with change-adept people convince them that the initiative is appropriate and necessary. Indeed, the best way to send the message of change throughout the organization is to translate it through the voices of people in the trenches.

Finally, it is crucial that the people doing the work within the organization accept and embrace the change initiative. The one sure way to measure whether this *transferability* has happened is to talk with the people on the level of the shop floor. If the message of the leader is echoed in the words used on the shop floor, then transferability has taken place. For example, if the leader has said that "We must be number one or number two in every market we serve," you will hear the entire organization paraphrasing that message. The words no longer belong to the leader; they now belong to the people who are doing the work. They own the Agenda for Change. And they will make it happen.

LEADERSHIP VERSUS MANAGEMENT

Understanding how a change message is transferred to the organization requires focusing on the important differences between leadership and management. It comes down to a fundamental distinction: formulating vision versus carrying out vision.

Jeff Otten acknowledges the strength of his managers as a key reason for the success of his Agenda for Change. As Jeff has observed, leadership by itself, without strong management, is not enough. Leadership and management are required together—in the correct mixture—for successful change implementation.

What is the difference between leadership and management? We all know people in leadership roles who are not leaders. I can readily think of numerous politicians, CEOs, and team captains who fit that description. Conversely, it is easy to call to mind people who are not in leadership roles and yet exhibit leadership qualities. Then there are those in leadership roles who exhibit tremendous skills as managers. And, finally, there are the managers who exhibit leadership skills but poor management ability. The bottom line is that the divisions between the qualities of leadership and management are frequently blurred. Regardless of formal title or position, people can be either leaders or managers, both, or neither.

The differences between leaders and managers are frequently found at the task level, where the work actually gets done. Managers are usually closer to the output and throughput of work systems, whereas leaders are frequently one or two steps removed from that type of detail. For managers, the work of project management includes designing work processes and systems, scheduling, organizing, reporting, and focusing on concepts such as scope of work, flowcharts, and human resource loading. Given a defined scope of work, a manager says specific things, makes strong commitments, and creates clarity around the necessary tasks. The manager also builds processes that tie together the necessary procedural steps to get the work done. His or her job is to tightly manage all elements of the project, work within the parameters of the design, and produce deliverables. In order to effectively do this, he or she strives to create a positive, efficient environment in which work can happen.

The work of a leader is different. The leader's role is to work outside the boundaries of the project environment itself, look for new and better ways to get the answers to questions that have been or will be asked, anticipate barriers and knock them down, and build roads through tangled jungles. The role of the leader is like that of a great sculptor who sees a figure hidden inside a rough piece of marble and sees the process of creating the piece as a liberation of what should and must come into existence. He or she minutely chips away at the rock, flake by flake, to realize that vision. Today, work is more complex and blurry. There is therefore a greater need than ever before for leaders who can see the figures in the marble and communicate that vision to those around them.

Leaders differ from managers in their approach to structures, lines, and boundaries. Managers, by the very nature of their roles, work within defined processes, which delineate their work; they need to function, operate, and execute in a very organized and clear way. Leaders, on the other hand, have the ability to work across boundaries, knock away artificial lines, see and connect natural synergies, and communicate inside and outside normal channels. High-Impact Leaders capitalize on this agility by having Powerful Conversations wherever, whenever, and with whoever in the organization it is most vital to do so.

Powerful Conversations, however, should not be construed to be solely within the domain of the leader—they are critical success factors for managers as well. There is an important difference, however. Managers have Powerful Conversations around critical work processes. They are focused on getting work done better, faster, and more effectively and tailor their Powerful Conversations accordingly. Leaders, of course, engage in Powerful Conversations of a broader scope. They are more focused on building trust, explaining the big picture, and enabling through the building of confidence and commitment. Sometimes, the distinction between a leader's

Powerful Conversations and a manager's Powerful Conversations blurs. It is nevertheless valuable to see the lines clearly drawn at least in the abstract to gain a better picture of the distinct challenges of leadership and management—and the importance of Powerful Conversations to each.

PASSIONATE CHAMPIONS

Jeff Otten is currently in Step Five of his Agenda for Change, continuing to ensure that there are Passionate Champions in key positions throughout the organization to drive the charge. We will deal in much greater detail in the next chapter about how High-Impact Leaders identify and deploy Passionate Champions. However, let me define the term now for our immediate purposes: a Passionate Champion is *a change agent whose personal mission is to achieve very specific change-related goals and who creates change in pursuit of his or her objectives.*

There are those who are change adept: they are comfortable with change and able to function well despite it. There are others who go further than that: they actually embrace change and thrive on it. These are the Passionate Champions. When given a task involving change or when empowered to create change, a Passionate Champion engages in a personal mission to make that change happen.

Imagine the power to be gained by enlisting the right people in an organization, regardless of title or role, to implement an overall Agenda for Change strategy. Such enlistment happens all the time during any successful change initiative. The difference in the process Jeff Otten undertook was that he used formal means to identify exactly who his Passionate Champions were, and then laid out a strategic approach to engaging with those individuals through Powerful Conversations in order to make the necessary connections and provide the Passionate Champions with the tools needed to make the change happen.

In other words, he fixed his bets in order to maximize his results. Wouldn't you? In order to achieve successful and lasting organizational transformation in only five years, Jeff had to do exactly that. Discovering, connecting, and enlisting Passionate Champions is the critical success factor in forging change that sticks.

TAKING AIM WITH A POWERFUL CONVERSATION: TARGETING CHANGE

For a senior leader burdened by complexities and the sheer number of people within his or her sphere of influence, it is absolutely vital to be focused, targeted, and strategic about the use of Powerful Conversations. Any given day brings a parade of people and a host of problems involved in the change process. There are only a certain number of Powerful Conversations a leader can take part in on a given day, however.

Alene Korby at Kraft Foods is one leader who recognizes the importance of picking the right targets and spots. Alene has transformed her group through the effective use of Powerful Conversations, but she initially found the use of this technology draining until she learned the principle of aiming Powerful Conversations at critically important areas. Alene's experience reminded me of a discussion I had in 1975 with Harry Loebel, who was then president of Raytheon Service Company. Harry said, "I spend 70 percent of my time with people who are not making it. All the problems are with people who cannot get through their own problems." So frequently in my discussions with senior leaders, no matter the industry, I hear the same complaint: "I'm bogged down with problem people."

But, is it the job of the leader to solve problems? I would submit that it is the job of the leader to move the organization forward and the job of the manager to address problems and keep the organization on track. The work of the leader should not involve "problem people." It should instead involve spending time with the people who will make the difference in achieving the organization's overall strategy. The leader should try to make these people feel motivated and connected to the organizational compass we call strategy.

Alene and I discussed the situation and worked from there to gain a finer understanding of the nuances between managers and leaders. She came to the realization that she didn't need to have a Powerful Conversation with every single person involved in her change initiative. It would simply be too exhausting, involving, and draining a process. High-Impact Leaders know that every single conversation doesn't need to be a Powerful Conversation.

This knowledge made Alene that much more effective as a High-Impact Leader. She realized she needed to function as a manager (and have management-focused Powerful Conversations) only when working within the confines of a project. Her work as leader, on the other hand, called for her to step outside the traditional relationship boundaries and go directly to the Passionate Champions most capable of and responsible for delivering specific results.

In the final analysis, whether you are a manager or leader (or both), it is only through slow accumulation that your Powerful Conversations will gain truly significant weight. If I have two to four Powerful Conversations a day for the roughly 250 workdays in the year, then I will have between

500 and 1000 impactful communications per year. Think of the power of that. If I have advanced my agenda, promoted learning, and strengthened relationships that many times in a year, then I am probably meeting most (if not all) of my leadership challenges.

ABANDONING THE CHAINS OF COMMAND:
THE LEADER AS FREE RADICAL

As Jeff Otten has discovered, leaders have more effective Powerful Conversations when they go around the chain of command, through the chain of command, and over the chain of command directly to the Passionate Champions. The reason Jeff Otten has been so successful is that he speaks directly to these Passionate Champions across the system. On a given day, Jeff could meet and talk with the chairs of medical disciplines, heads of various clinics, and any of 450 managers. The greatest impact he can have and does have on a day-to-day basis, however, is in his interactions with Passionate Champions.

By going beyond formal boundaries and aiming Powerful Conversations deliberately, High-Impact Leaders create maximum impact. The role of a leader in implementing an Agenda for Change is all about aiming energy at high-return targets. This doesn't mean Powerful Conversations should only take place outside traditional chains of command, because that is clearly not the case. Rather, the point is that Powerful Conversations are not limited by structure, hierarchy, or chain of command. Unfortunately, the "leader as free radical" situation does not occur enough in the real world, which is far more comfortable with chains of communication and linking people together by formal means. But real communication does not necessarily flow through such an even pipeline, no matter how rationally and logically it is connected.

When it comes to implementing an Agenda for Change, High-Impact Leaders have their greatest impact when they target their communication around Passionate Champions. And the best organizations consciously make sure this type of communication happens. At Cisco Systems in San Jose, California, senior leaders spend a significant amount of their time talking with Passionate Champions throughout the organization—and make a point of doing so on a daily basis. Senior leaders at Cisco and other organizations have that type of freedom.

In general, the higher the level of a person inside of an organization, the more leeway and opportunity he or she has to have Powerful Conversations at the closest levels to the work being done. Too many senior leaders, however, are too far removed from the actual work of the enterprise. This is due in large part to the widely held belief that the work of leaders at higher levels involves interacting with only the next level of leadership. But it doesn't have to be this way. High-Impact Leaders spend as much time as possible staying in close contact with the people doing the real work of the organization. They simply don't allow themselves to get cocooned. Imagine having senior leaders inside of an organization acting as a team deployed across the boundaries of the organization in an effort to create impact on the Passionate Champions responsible for delivering major programs, products, and projects. How valuable would it be to have Powerful Conversations regarding purpose, strategy, and new and better ways to get to higher levels of learning for the organization—thereby impacting overall and specific goal achievement?

The challenge for High-Impact Leaders today is to focus their organizations on an Agenda for Change that they are trying to advance. A leader cannot accomplish this unless he or she has the managers in place inside the organization driving that agenda—and unless he or she is able to reach the Passionate Champions who can drive the major work efforts that will make a difference. By pulling organizational learning into this concept (as Jeff Otten did in Step Four of BWH's Agenda for Change), you develop a model that creates a permanently focused and controlled change process for continually advancing organizational effectiveness. The critical success factor for this model is the strategic and disciplined use of Powerful Conversations.

C H A P T E R 8

PASSIONATE CHAMPIONS

ONE OF THE GREAT lessons of leadership is that you can't do it by yourself. In the preceding chapter, we focused on using Powerful Conversations in a systematic, strategic, and targeted way to implement an Agenda for Change. Passionate Champions are the link between designing an Agenda for Change and implementing it. They assist a High-Impact Leader in ensuring that the organization will effectively embrace change and achieve the corrective objectives of the Agenda for Change. They are the missionaries of believability, turning achievability into transferability.

In this chapter, we will look in much closer detail at who Passionate Champions are, how they can be identified, and what processes are needed to bring these people's passionately felt wants and needs into alignment with Agenda for Change goals. Passionate Champions always stand out because of the strength of their drive and sense of responsibility for change; linking that drive to the leader's Agenda for Change through Powerful Conversations is the key to achieving organizational change objectives.

PASSIONATE CHAMPIONS DEFINED

As we described in the last chapter, a Passionate Champion is a change agent whose personal mission is to achieve very specific change-related goals and who creates change in pursuit of his or her objectives. Passionate Champions usually have the following characteristics:

- They are highly driven and enormously focused, with strong mental discipline.
- They are trusted inside of organizations; everyone knows how committed they are to getting specific tasks accomplished.
- They see the big picture, but they don't often invent.
- They are not necessarily systems thinkers but they are always perceptive.
- They are achievement oriented.
- They are drivers, capable of creating unstoppable momentum—although they are not necessarily extroverted or introverted (personality type doesn't matter).
- They simply don't entertain the probabilities of *not* reaching their objectives.

Passionate Champions are driven by the challenge to win against all odds. They will do whatever it takes within a value structure to get things done. They are willing to do what few will do to reach a goal. They are, in short, thoroughbreds. The negative side is that they will leave organizations that are not willing to support their own agendas or make them feel aligned with the leader's agenda. When properly engaged, though, Passionate Champions have an extremely positive impact: they convince others of the importance of achieving whatever goal they are striving for.

I have never had trouble explaining the concept of Passionate Champions to leaders. Within seconds, they can usually think of several people within their organizations who qualify as Passionate Champions. High-Impact Leaders recognize the need for and value of effectively enlisting such people to their overall cause. As a strategic concept for obtaining maximum results, using Passionate Champions is a no-brainer.

The difficulty lies in keeping Passionate Champions focused and committed, not only to their own immediate, work-related goals but also to the goals of the organization's Agenda for Change. Passionate Champions are, by nature, renegades and lone rangers, more naturally inclined to their own agendas than to yours. They are, in fact, frequently misaligned with the organization's agenda. They are innovative freethinkers. Unharnessed, these people can become destructive forces rather than constructive missionaries of change and improvement.

High-Impact Leaders use Powerful Conversations to connect Passionate Champions to the Agenda for Change. And that is the key to driving an Agenda for Change throughout an organization.

EMPOWERMENT VERSUS ENLISTMENT

Engaging with a Passionate Champion is not about empowerment, at least in the traditional sense. *Empowerment* is, in many respects, an overused and misused word. As a concept, because it differs from the way organizations actually function, empowerment is vulnerable to ridicule and appropriately maligned in comic strips like *Dilbert*. It sounds good in theory to say that you are "empowering" people, but most leaders I know are unwilling to risk their agendas by sacrificing that much control. And with good reason: there is no doubt that, given free reign, Passionate Champions would pursue their own agendas. And those agendas probably wouldn't line up with yours or your organization's. Herein lies the difference, the source of dissatisfaction, *and* the opportunity for tapping the tremendous energy of a Passionate Champion.

In all honesty, High-Impact Leaders are much less interested in empowerment than they are in control. If the fastest and most effective way to get a job done were to command others to take specific actions, High-Impact Leaders would be the first to do so. But command and control work less well than selling someone on the genuine need for something—and High-Impact Leaders know it. That's why they use Powerful Conversations. By attracting, motivating, and retaining special individuals who happen to have their own unique agendas, leaders can promote their own interests as well.

In order to do this effectively, the High-Impact Leader must understand what a Passionate Champion is all about. Let me relay a story that illustrates the value of using Powerful Conversations to drive Passionate Champions within an organization.

FORMING A TEAM OF PASSIONATE CHAMPIONS

Pat Taylor was a rising star in an integrated energy company. She specialized in turning around groups or departments that needed to radically rethink the way they operated in response to deregulation of the industry. She had been particularly successful in the natural gas side of the business in the UK, where markets were wide open and the company competed aggressively.

Pat leaped at the chance to join the fuel supply department of the global company's plants in the American Midwest. Deregulation in many key energy markets was imminent. As head of coal purchasing, Pat was eager to face the challenges presented by the volume of the business and the massiveness of the change. The senior team of coal buyers who led the department was among the best negotiations teams in the business. Its members were methodical and careful, but they were used to big deals and had great confidence. Pat was looking forward to working with such a high-performing team.

It was a different matter when she came on board. Pat completely underestimated the conservative culture of this new group and its deeply entrenched approach to operations. In particular, the old boys' network of coal buyers was not interested in hearing about new strategies from someone who had cut her teeth in natural gas markets in the UK.

Seeing what needed to be done was the easy part. Pat had worked in deregulated units before and she knew what the Agenda for Change needed to be as soon as she walked in the door. Getting buy-in from the key leaders in the department, however, seemed next to impossible. She was new and an outsider, and, as people pointed out to her time and again, she didn't know coal markets. To her senior team, the nature of the commodity and the way it was bought and shipped required operations to work in a certain way for a reason.

Pat benchmarked the industry. It was true, even according to rival coal companies, that the team's negotiating skills were among the best in the business. But costs had already been driven down to bare minimum. Leaders in the coal industry itself were transforming in order to prepare for new ways of doing business. They were eager to operate differently and saw all the money that could be made in more open markets. Creating alliances between suppliers and purchasers was the key to survival and growth going forward. Negotiating could no longer be an "us versus them" way of business.

Still, Pat delayed in pushing through with her strategy. The changes to come would be disruptive enough without running roughshod over her new team. Even though senior management had brought her on board to make big changes, for months she did nothing.

Pat knew she had to approach change in a different way. We talked about Passionate Champions as a way of making it happen. Together, we plotted out a strategy for bringing the organization into line with the Agenda for Change despite the resistance of the highest-ranking members of the team. Pat's success reveals the power of Passionate Champions as agents of change.

She decided that she could no longer waste time with the members of the coal buying team; their ways were set. In order to get the department to operate differently, she would have to go around the team and work with the department directly. She announced her intentions to do so to the coal buying team, hoping this would serve as a wake-up call. She was going to seek out the change-adept people in the organization and make the Agenda for Change happen.

Disregarding who reported to whom, Pat reached out to those people in the 250-person department who were open to change. Some were directors and project managers, others were administrative assistants. From Pat's own personal knowledge of the members of the department, she assessed them in stages by identifying

1.   Those who demonstrated motivation and energy
2.   Those who possessed the highest levels of ability at their jobs
3.   Those who were skilled at influencing and persuading others

In interviews with these people, she determined that they had high Focused Drive and that they maintained commitments passionately. They had many success stories about overcoming challenges, and they were well liked by immediate colleagues, having in essence cultivated their own networks of supporters. As individuals they had been frequently at odds with the goals of the department, but in discussing visions for how the industry could be transformed, Pat could see that their agendas could be woven in with hers. During the interviews, Pat felt that a personal connection happened between them, partly because she recognized their abilities, partly because they all saw the need for change.

From Pat's big picture perspective, these people's individual agendas weren't of much help to the whole department. It was their ability to drive forward with a new approach that made them valuable for her in achieving the overall Agenda for Change. She made them her Passionate Champion team and designated each of them as head of a task group formed to work on different aspects for a new way of doing business.

The changes, the results, the shake-up of the department, and the wins came together more quickly than anyone (including Pat) anticipated. In fact, Pat's main difficulty quickly became putting into place the infrastructure needed to build the new processes that people now hungered for. Aligning the agendas of ten Passionate Champions out of a large department created a revolutionary energy for change. Eventually, the movement broke the resistance of the coal buying team. There was a gradual loosening up of the team members' hardened mind-sets. They started to see things differently. They became more enthusiastic about the new process improvements and began to implement them.

ALIGNING AGENDAS

Passionate Champions are of little value unless they become aligned to the Agenda for Change process within an organization. If Passionate Champions are not pulled into the initiative, they end up unaligned or misaligned, and are bound to expend their tremendous energy at cross-purposes to the organization's overall strategy.

Although Passionate Champions may occupy important positions in the chain of command, they are just as frequently outside of it. More often than not, a Passionate Champion asserts responsibility informally. He or she is the person who will grab the reins of a project, idea, task, or objective because he or she feels strongly about it. One tremendous benefit of Passionate Champions is that they assume your worry. John Keane, President of Keane, Inc., says to his Passionate Champions, "If you are worried, then I don't have to be."

Although the importance of seeking change-adept people outside of the structured hierarchy is talked about in many management classes and leadership books, doing so is a difficult concept for most leaders in practice. High-Impact Leaders, however, are skilled at finding and working with people outside of the formal chains of command. If there is really such a thing as empowerment, I think it comes about precisely in that way—from communicating directly with the people in the organization who are most capable and actively aligning their goals with those of the organization. Aligning Passionate Champions with the Agenda for Change ensures that the passion of the Agenda for Change process is amplified and transferred widely.

Some leaders are risk averse and are hesitant to bring in Passionate Champions. They worry that Passionate Champions don't fit inside the organization or aren't predictable in buying into an agenda. The real risk, however, lies in the failure to enlist Passionate Champions. Without them, a change initiative, no matter how well planned or conceived, will have little chance of success.

Success with Passionate Champions is ensured only through Powerful Conversations. Identifying Passionate Champions is one challenge—but a challenge you can meet rather easily once you understand the common traits and characteristics of Passionate Champions. The real difficulty lies in being able to capture the attention and harness the energy of Passionate Champions. In a sense, this is all about connecting the agenda of the Passionate Champion with the overall Agenda for Change.

In organizing Passionate Champions, it is necessary to convince them to focus on the big picture agenda for a while. Most often Passionate Champions will do so only because they see that it fits with their agendas and will bring them benefits such as recognition, satisfaction, and financial reward. It is always difficult to keep a Passionate Champion on board. Powerful Conversations are a must in this regard because they can continually and reliably get to the heart of a Passionate Champion's real wants and needs.

While Passionate Champions are willing to buy into someone else's organizational frame, they frequently feel that they are out there by themselves and that their drive and passion are unrecognized and considered to be not only radical, but also unacceptable. When High-Impact Leaders tie them into an overall strategy, Passionate Champions are eager to open up and express their own hidden thoughts. They appreciate it when the leader genuinely reveals that he or she understands, accepts, and needs the Passionate Champion. Connecting in such a special way makes the Passionate Champion feel a sense of incredible loyalty and respect toward the leader.

As a further example of the difficulty of aligning a Passionate Champion's agenda with an organizational agenda, consider the following story from the health care world. The CEO of a prestigious hospital in the Midwest was interviewing a candidate for the position of chair and director of cardiac surgery. The position had long been a big concern for the CEO. For a year and a half, there had been no leader in place—which might have been an improvement over the prior director, given that he had dug in around the very cost reduction effort that was a top item on the CEO's Agenda for Change. At this point, though, the CEO felt that he had to fill the position as quickly as possible.

There was one candidate in particular who, in terms of sheer talent, was the right person for the job. The CEO knew the candidate was a superstar, someone who had a reputation for getting things done. At the same time, the candidate was also regarded as a maverick and even a lone ranger. But the CEO knew that, properly harnessed, the surgeon could be of enormous value to the organization. So he decided in the interview to put everything on the line and tell the candidate then and there about his Agenda for Change. He did so to ensure from the beginning that their relationship was open and committed to the same mutual goals.

"Doctor, I want you to know that you are considered to be a world-class physician, a great research-minded strategist with a rock-solid reputation inside of academic medical centers wherever you have been," the CEO said. "I'll be honest from the outset. We would very much like for you to consider joining our staff. We are looking for someone who can and will drive the organization's agenda around cost reductions and care advancements. These are serious times. We need to cut 20 percent of our costs over the next two to three years and we need your commitment and buy-in to do it. If you are interested in this position, I want your help to get us there."

The surgeon confirmed that he was aware that he was known as an aggressive proponent of cardiac surgery and academic medicine. He also seemed to buy into the CEO's goals. "If you're interested in having me join you," he said, "I will do everything in my power to ensure that we can cut reasonable costs within the safe guidelines of high-quality medicine. From my perspective, since I haven't worked inside your organization, I don't know your cost structure and I'm unaware of the overall strategy. But I'm a team player and I'll do everything possible, whenever possible, to drive costs down, without endangering the safety and health of patients or the reputation of the organization."

It was more than the CEO had hoped for, and he was thrilled. He should have been upset. Indeed, the two participants in this conversation had been talking about two different agendas. Although it went through the surface motions of a Powerful Conversation, the interaction was actually chock-full of errors in assumption and unclear expressions of commitment.

Everyone who interviewed the surgeon felt he was exactly right for the organization's culture. The CEO made an offer and was surprised when the candidate rejected it. As he later asked me, "He gave us every signal that he liked what we stood for. What went wrong?"

In reviewing this specific interview further with the CEO, here is what we discovered. Regarding alignment of agendas, it was absolutely critical that the CEO first understood the agenda of his candidate without making assumptions. He needed to honestly unveil the candidate's feelings and passions, and explore where those lines intersected, in order to have any chance at getting to mutual commitments around each other's agendas. This he did not do.

In reality, the candidate had a terrible reputation when it came to driving down costs. The CEO was led to believe, through his own hopes, that this time would be different. The language the candidate used was actually very clear, however. What he was really saying was, "I will not compromise patient quality care for cost reduction. I have a hang-up with institutions that are focusing on cost when they should be focusing on quality. I abhor standards that are set around costs and am unwilling to compromise cost for quality care." Instead the CEO became convinced, after hearing phrases like "balancing quality with cost," that he and the candidate were talking about the same things. They were not.

Fortunately, after coaching on how to get and perform a rebounding interview, the CEO was able to go back to this surgeon and have a Powerful Conversation. This time, the CEO took the opportunity to explore in more detail why the surgeon was passionate about the work he had chosen to do. They talked about what the surgeon felt most deeply about and believed in through stories of past experiences that exemplified those feelings.

After building up a certain rapport and comfort level, the CEO opened up and became more direct about his wants and needs. He told the surgeon the history of what had happened in the hospital regarding costs and the barriers this had put up to achieving the objectives of the organization. He had listened closely to the candidate's stories, and now he used them in relaying his own concerns and goals. After paraphrasing the candidate's biggest concerns to make sure he was correct in his assumptions, the CEO opened up a discussion focused on how they could both potentially meet their goals. This time, it was a discussion that had both of them excited about working together.

Together (in that one session, in fact), they outlined how they could spread the Agenda for Change through the entire academic medical system, so that doctors, nurses, clinical professionals, administrators, patients, and families would all react positively to the change initiative. It was a conversation that secured the candidate's fullest commitments and most passionate energies, and one well worth the second effort.

As this story illustrates, it is always necessary to hook Passionate Champions into the Agenda for Change of the organization in ways that go beyond lip service buy-in. It is equally true that you cannot get buy-in for your Agenda for Change unless you share in the passion of the Passionate Champion's agenda. In fact, only by investing such time and energy into that person's agenda can you get to your own. By doing this, a High-Impact Leader sends a clear message that he or she is totally interested in the Passionate Champion's agenda, contributing clarity about what he or she is willing to commit to in support of that agenda. This becomes the foundation of a burgeoning trust and the reason the Passionate Champion stays connected to the goals of the organization.

ENSURING THAT PASSIONATE CHAMPIONS STAY ALIGNED
Time, commitment, and communication are the keys to ensuring that Passionate Champions stay successful inside of organizations.

Trust comes about through the fulfillment of a series of commitments and is easily shattered when High-Impact Leaders don't have the time, don't live their commitments, or fail to communicate on a regular basis with Passionate Champions. By their very nature, Passionate Champions are self-motivated and self-directed. Still, they require the nourishment that comes from personal interactions to keep them aligned. Passionate Champions need to know that they have the backing and support of their leaders.

Here are some of the techniques I have seen High-Impact Leaders use to ensure that Passionate Champions remain nourished.

1.   *High-Impact Leaders spend quality time with Passionate Champions on a regular basis.* A number of years ago, Tom Peters became

famous for the concept of strategically walking around to touch base with those in the organization responsible for driving change. Such a strategy is inadequate and insufficient to meet the needs of the Passionate Champion. Passionate Champions need uninterrupted, focused time involving total listening about what is going with them, what they want, and what they need to succeed. High-Impact Leaders recognize this and spend time with Passionate Champions, both during business hours and away from the job. The latter is difficult today, and yet it is one of the most important ways High-Impact Leaders stay connected with Passionate Champions.

2. *High-Impact Leaders frequently check in with Passionate Champions to ensure that they stay on track.* The biggest single complaint from Passionate Champions in the workplace remains, "My leader takes for granted that I know what he or she is thinking. I feel that I am all alone in my task and that my capabilities and heroic efforts are taken for granted." Because Passionate Champions are distribution channels for information and enthusiasm, the more time spent in communication with Passionate Champions, the clearer the message and more articulate the Agenda for Change will be for the organization at large. When Passionate Champions don't feel aligned, they are more inclined to ignore or, in the worst-case scenario, badmouth the Agenda for Change process. And an antagonistic Passionate Champion inside the organization is ten times more destructive than the average disgruntled employee. Passionate Champions are respected by their peers. When they are discouraged and misaligned, chances are they will infect rather than inoculate the organization to resist the change initiative.

3. *High-Impact Leaders follow up on the commitments they make to their Passionate Champions.* At the end of every conversation with a Passionate Champion, it is especially critical to confirm commitments and assumptions. High-Impact Leaders are also careful to tell Passionate Champions when they can't get them something. Above all, High-Impact Leaders, when dealing with Passionate Champions, do not pay lip service to an agreement. Breaking promises will inevitably cause a Passionate Champion to revert to his or her own agenda at the organization's expense.

HOW MANY PASSIONATE CHAMPIONS DO YOU NEED?

Ideally, you would like as many Passionate Champions as you can get to support your Agenda for Change. It is important to remember, however, that handling Passionate Champions consumes significant time and energy. Thus, you need only as many as you can handle effectively to drive your Agenda for Change.

The way to attain the right number of Passionate Champions is to think about it as a progressive process. Passionate Champions can be added one by one to a reservoir of like-minded people, making the role of the leader easier and easier. The need for Passionate Champions diminishes as the achievability, believability, and transferability of the Agenda for Change spreads. When the Agenda for Change is no longer a priority for the organization, Passionate Champions can become dormant, existing in reduced capacity at various positions and levels throughout the organization, waiting for the next urgent call from the High-Impact Leader.

High-Impact Leaders build webs of Passionate Champions to drive change throughout an organization. They do it patiently and carefully, using Powerful Conversations to listen closely to wants and needs. They spend the time and make the efforts to get to know Passionate Champions in a special way to find the connection that will allow a transfer and exchange of beliefs and feelings.

In a sense, what really happens between Passionate Champions and High-Impact Leaders is a bonding of mutually agreed self-interests. They support each other's agendas in a way that creates shared focus and affects the organization at large. Together, they resolve to truly make a difference.

It is the transfer of energy, enthusiasm, and emotion that allows the High-Impact Leader to align the Passionate Champion within the Agenda for Change process. On the other side of the equation, the Passionate Champion emerges with trust and a belief that the High-Impact Leader will support him or her. The Passionate Champion now can win. And these people exist to win.

High-Impact Leaders don't waste time trying to make every person in the organization a Passionate Champion. They aim their Powerful Conversations selectively—toward those who have the passion to create change. They also insulate Passionate Champions, so that they don't become confused, disorganized, or prey to bureaucratic tendencies. They make sure the Passionate Champions get what they need so that they stay aligned. It is the ability to keep Passionate Champions aligned that creates unstoppable momentum for the High-Impact Leader's Agenda for Change.

RETAINING
GREAT PEOPLE

THERE IS A WAR for talent going on. High-Impact Leaders recognize the necessity of getting the best people and keeping them. They know how to identify which employees are their top performers, representing their most important assets. At the same time, they resist the temptation of labeling every single employee as key. With respect to the true top performers, they do not take loyalty and commitment for granted. And they make sure the top performers around them are connected to organizational goals in order to increase levels of retention.

In today's competitive environment, it is critical to become realistic about what drives retention and to develop retention plans that recognize the particular needs and wants of star performers. High-Impact Leaders today are forging their own retention practices by talking to key employees and asking them directly what they want and need in the short and long term. From the outset, they ask, "What will it take to keep you motivated, interested, and linked?" Powerful Conversations help you connect with your best people in ways that inspire them to work with you, not against you. Before we explore this more fully, let's first examine some basic facts about turnover.

THE REALITY ABOUT TURNOVER
In its simplest terms, turnover is the loss of a human resource that requires a replacement. There are two kinds of turnover: planned and unplanned.

Planned turnover—when someone retires or has to move on or over—is usually not a problem. Unplanned turnover, on the other hand, can be, and frequently is, devastating to organizations. When a key person leaves, it can create tremendous hurt and dislocation, result in lost business and lower margins, and, in rare cases, put an organization out of business. In today's world of knowledge workers, where there is a scarcity of critical human assets, unplanned turnover can be downright scary.

The more successful organizations hold on to their key people because they know unplanned turnover can end up costing as much as three to five times the annual salaries of the individuals involved. We are at the dawn of an era of increasing instability, one in which many knowledge-based industries will likely show a 30 to 40 percent rate of annual turnover. The rules are changing as to why employees leave and what companies are prepared to do to keep employees who are threatening to leave.

Consider that on any given day, while your organization is hard at work defining new and better ways to attract new talent, headhunters are at your back door talking to your key talent, encouraging these people to consider better opportunities elsewhere. What recruiters look for in their cold calling and referral networks are *dissatisfiers,* a term we will explore more fully later in this chapter. They know from experience that they can convince any employee, even the best and most loyal, to focus on what is not right with his or her organization. So the recruiters present new possibilities of what is "more right," what is a better fit, and where to go to get more satisfaction. It follows that organizations—and the High-Impact Leaders that lead them—need to understand better what makes employees leave their organizations. To do so, let's look at how the process begins. Let's examine how top performers are convinced at the outset to leave one organization and join another.

RECRUITING THE BEST

Many years ago, when I was the employment manager for a division of Raytheon Company, I observed that certain leaders had a higher rate of success in recruiting quality candidates. These leaders seemed to connect with applicants in a meaningful fashion during the interviews.

I asked the leaders with the highest acceptance rates what they said during their interviews and how they conducted them. What was their secret? Over and over, I heard phrases like: "I tell them how I honestly feel about the organization," "I ask them about themselves," "I tell them about me," "Once I click with a person, I dig deeper," "I'm up-front about specific commitments," and "I don't hide a thing."

I know now that these leaders were using the technique of Powerful Conversations. High-Impact Leaders create trust during job interviews by spending a great deal of time relating to the applicant through honest dialogue. They also manage to demonstrate caring. And they share freely of themselves, so that the applicant feels assured that everything said in the interview is true. After this connection takes place, High-Impact Leaders discuss what the job entails. Here, they do not rely on the formal job description. Instead, they are clear about customers, contexts, outputs, challenges, and opportunities. They define the skills and behaviors that are needed. They also discuss the performance standards of success. Finally, they use stories to provide a vivid picture of the organization and its culture.

I reached these conclusions by studying the master recruiters at Raytheon. And I learned an important lesson from my investigation. It has to do with what I call *satisfiers*—the needs and wants the applicant has with respect to the job. There are six primary satisfiers, each revolving around a central underlying question:

Satisfier	*Underlying question*
Work/role	Do the job functions, tasks, responsibilities, and competencies fit my needs and expectations?
Salary/benefits	Does the remuneration match both my expectations/needs and what the marketplace will pay?
Career development	Will the level of potential learning and growth meet my expectations (and market expectations)?
Team	Will I fit/relate to the team, and will I be accepted by the team members?
Culture	Will the values, operating principles, and beliefs of the organization fit mine?
Work/life	Will the job permit me to strike an acceptable balance between work and personal life?

These are broad categories, of course. Within them, each individual has particular wants, needs, and desires as to what will satisfy him or her. But these six satisfiers nevertheless broadly capture what attracts applicants to a particular job or organization—and what keeps them in place after they arrive.

During the interview process, the candidate should be trying to determine whether enough of his or her satisfiers are present—and the interviewer should be looking to prove that these satisfiers are indeed present so that the applicant will accept the position. Unfortunately, what happens in most interviews is that both participants play their cards carefully. Applicant and interviewer alike are so afraid of saying the wrong thing that they don't want to run the risk of putting satisfiers on the table. High-Impact Leaders, however, know the importance of uncovering and addressing a candidate's satisfiers during the interview. Through the use of Powerful Conversation technology, they inquire about the candidate's unique needs and wants. They continuously assess where a person stands, from first contact in the interview through the entire employment cycle after he or she joins the organization.

In the recruiting and retention wars, High-Impact Leaders know that all applicants and employees are at risk when their satisfiers are not being fulfilled. Whether he or she consciously knows it or not, each person has a set of assumptions about their satisfiers. Applicants usually have a checklist of satisfiers in mind. During the interview, they mentally keep track of which ones are likely to be met. If they conclude that several satisfiers will not be fulfilled, they will not accept the position. It is the interviewer's job to identify those satisfiers so that the organization can meet them. If that is not possible, then the interviewer will save the applicant (and the organization) lots of heartache by breaking things off right then and there.

But assuming you can meet someone's satisfiers, how do you convince the best people to join you and not someone else? Rick Pitino, currently the head coach and president of the Boston Celtics, believes it rests on the quality of the connection. It is not just about how well you explain your organization and your goals. It is equally important how well you listen to the candidate and understand his or her goals.

When Pitino coached at Providence College and the University of Kentucky, he took recruiting players as seriously as any other part of the job. The importance of getting the best talent is glaringly important to success in college basketball. The same is true in business.

Recognizing this importance, Pitino would spend inordinate amounts of time with high school scouting reports studying the profiles of potential candidates for his team. He did everything he could to understand as much as possible about a player he was trying to recruit. And he didn't limit his investigation to a player's performance on the court—he also tried to learn about the player's family and his interests. Armed with that knowledge, Pitino would frequently call and ask if he could visit and have dinner with the player and his family. Pitino would use that occasion to draw a picture of what life would be like at his institution and what it would be like to play basketball for Rick Pitino. The picture he painted was a realistic one. He knew it was necessary to be up-front and clear about the hard work and commitments involved with playing on his team. Pitino was an especially demanding college coach who drove his players, and he wanted a recruit to know that from the start.

Sometimes, his approach didn't work. On one particular occasion, he could tell just from looking in a recruit's eyes that, despite Pitino's thorough preparation and his most sincere efforts at connection, the player wasn't going to join him. He realized right then that it was because the player wanted something and Pitino didn't know what it was. From that day on, Pitino changed his approach to recruiting. He learned that it was necessary to take his recruiting conversations to a new level—to practice what we have termed Powerful Conversations.

In business, Powerful Conversations greatly facilitate the interview process because they force a High-Impact Leader to listen, connect, and define commitments. You cannot really open someone up to sharing his or her own beliefs until you have made a clear connection with that person. But when the connection is made and stories begin to emerge, a skillful interviewer probes to identify satisfiers. Sometimes these are lifestyle issues like work hours. Sometimes they are focused on achievements and how success is rewarded. With a firm understanding of where each of you stands, you can come to commitments that are livable, not hollow.

RETAINING THE BEST

Now let's turn our attention away from recruiting to the flip side: retention. There are various reasons employees leave one employer for another. As one recruiter recently remarked to me, "Employees never leave because of just one dissatisfier." This statement may represent a generalization, but it speaks volumes about the reality of turnover. Indeed, while some employees leave an organization because there are multiple upsides in a potential new job, many others leave just to get out. Such a desperation strategy is the result of two or more dissatisfiers associated with the old job. Even in cases where there are large financial advances, key employees are unlikely to leave just for the money. Undoubtedly, there is a price point at which we are all willing to take the leap, but we have talked to hundreds who have turned down huge cash upsides because "it simply wasn't right." Dissatisfiers are what drive them away.

Earlier, we identified certain satisfiers. Now we are speaking of dissatisfiers. In reality, satisfiers and dissatisfiers are merely different sides of the same coin. Satisfiers convince people to join and stay at an organization. Dissatisfiers are slightly different: they are the factors that cause people to leave the organization. There are five such dissatisfiers, which I will identify shortly. For now, let me relay a story that reveals how the presence of dissatisfiers can drive top performers away.

One of my clients, a managing director at a Wall Street investment banking firm, called me in a panic. One of her top equity analysts had just told her he was leaving. This man was only in his early thirties but was nevertheless invaluable to the firm. He was in the elite group of ranked equity analysts who, through their study of industries and companies and the corresponding reports they generate, can greatly impact the value of stocks, sometimes by as much as 50 percent. In addition, these top analysts are critical in generating new accounts for their firms. The backbone of any successful Wall Street institution is its research, and ranked equity analysts are the key to quality research.

"He's packing up his office right now. Can you hop on the next plane?" my client asked. I caught the shuttle from Boston to New York and was there a few hours later. Fortunately, I already had a relationship with the analyst from previous work I had done with the company on a model for high performance. Now, I sat with him and used the Tower of Power as a tool to discover what was driving his actions. "A lot of people are feeling badly about your leaving," I said. "You're critically important and a top producer. There's a need to understand what you need and want and didn't get. What commitments should be made to you and others for the future? Why are you leaving?"

He took his time in responding. "Do you really want me to tell you?" he asked. There was a lot of reluctance in his tone but I was obviously and aggressively pursuing the truth. I wanted to uncover the roots of his dissatisfaction. He went on to explain, "I wasn't taken seriously when it came to my impact on this team and I never got feedback. I'd be surprised if anyone knows what I wanted because no one ever asked."

It turned out that he wanted more resources and more staff to dig out research. He was also resentful of the bureaucracy of the organization. There were too many meetings and approvals required to do what he knew needed to be done. He wanted more respect for his own decision making ability. His youth, he felt, was holding him back at the firm, despite the business he generated.

He was making $5 million per year. The rumors were that he had been bought off, lured by a rival firm willing to spend the cash in its raid for talent. I asked him outright, "Are you leaving for the money?" It turned out that the new firm's package did indeed include a larger salary, but he told me that the money was not the dealmaker. It was the other factors. I asked if there were any way he would stay if the firm could find a way to address his dissatisfiers, but it was too late—he'd lost his trust in the institution and was skeptical that things could genuinely change.

The firm lost that guy, and I felt terrible about it, but I joined the firm's leaders in turning the episode into a learning opportunity and a great win for the organization. We started by meeting with the other managing directors worldwide to address the breakdown in communication. We used the Tower of Power to unearth the underlying assumptions and found that the company would (and did) pay competitive salaries to these analysts. At the same time, at a pittance of the relative cost, the firm had been reluctant to hire the research assistants requested by the analysts. We vowed to ramp up on those resources. We also set up a series of Powerful Conversations with the remaining top analysts to determine the unique sets of satisfiers of each. Eventually, we synthesized this information, put it on a matrix, and began using it as a guidepost in retaining top analysts. At the end of the process, the firm significantly improved its turnover in that position, one of the most difficult to keep filled on Wall Street.

Retention of key employees has become a critical factor in any organization's success. With employment levels at record highs, there is a growing emphasis and concern for attracting and keeping valuable personnel. Employers from all segments of industry are searching for hard-to-find resources and designing new and improved compensation and benefits packages to differentiate their organizations and make them more desirable. Companies will not only have a more difficult time in attracting employees, but also in keeping them. The stakes are enormous. Indeed, in the end, the "winners" at the retention game will own the human assets necessary to drive new business opportunities.

THE SIX MYTHS OF TURNOVER

Still, many leaders are playing according to the old rules. They cling to a certain mythology that has emerged regarding retention. Specifically, we have uncovered six primary myths that impede leaders in controlling turnover.

> *Myth One: People will stay because they are loyal to the organization.*
> Many leaders bank on "company loyalty" to keep their best talent
> in house, believing that employees will reject the gifts being
> thrown at their feet by talent raiders in the name of loyalty. To a

large extent, however, company loyalty is a thing of the past. This is due to the fact that today's fluid market economy encourages employee movement. There is no such thing as a "company man" or a "company woman" anymore; the loyalty is to your career, not your company. The best leaders recognize this and do not rely on "company loyalty" as a misguided strategy to retain talent.

Myth Two: All employees have a price and will leave if they get it. Many leaders believe that people will leave if they can get more money—and that this is the only reason they leave. For sure, money is always a factor in a departure decision. But, as shown in the analyst's story, money is never the sole factor and rarely the controlling factor. For instance, if the satisfiers noted earlier (namely work/role, salary/benefits, career development, team, culture, and work/life) are generally present, a person will probably stay put, even if it means turning down a job that offers more money. Conversely, if some of the specific dissatisfiers that we will identify shortly are present, a person will probably leave, even if it means taking a pay cut to do so. It's never just about the money.

Myth Three: Turnover is governed by demographic influences and is difficult to control in certain industries. Many who buy into this myth believe, for instance, that Generation Xers are more likely to leave than Baby Boomers. While this may be true to some degree, the generational focus is misplaced. Anyone can leave, regardless of age or generation. Similarly, while some industries are more prone to turnover, no industry is immune from large numbers of employees bolting. There are simply too many opportunities across all industries in this volatile age.

Myth Four: The departure of key people is a surprise. Key people always give out signals concerning their dissatisfiers, letting leaders know that things are not right for a period of time, right up until they decide to depart. Their departure, then, is never really a surprise. Still, when questioned, leaders often say that it was a surprise. Some leaders are more honest—they will admit that the signs were there all along and that they simply failed to pay attention to them. Failing to read the signs is a tragic flaw.

Myth Five: Turnover is a series of isolated cases that occur in a vacuum. In fact, once the revolving door begins to swing, it quickly picks up momentum and will take a number of the dissatisfied in its wake. Leaders frequently make the mistake of doing nothing when a key person leaves, believing that things will quickly get back to normal. Turnover, we find, usually happens in bunches. It can become like a virus that spreads through a department, division, or organization. The best leaders talk about a key departure, deal with the loss, and then focus on keeping other top performers on board.

Myth Six: The overall turnover rate is the important measure. Some leaders consciously strive for, say, a 10 percent turnover rate rather than a rate of 20 percent. The actual rate, however, is less significant than the particular people who actually leave. This is not to discount the sheer numbers in the turnover equation, because a mass exodus can have a huge impact, particularly if it is not planned. In the final analysis, though, how many you lose matters less than who you lose. Put another way, it's better to lose 20 mediocre people than five top performers.

DISSATISFIERS

High-Impact Leaders reject these myths of turnover and focus instead on the true challenges associated with retention. They also recognize that Powerful Conversations are critical to winning the game of retention. Such communication allows High-Impact Leaders to stay in touch with their top performers and preserve these people's loyalty and commitment.

Most employees, in fact, really don't want to leave their organizations. When specific dissatisfiers arise, however, they feel they must leave. Specifically, we have observed that employees typically leave because of the presence of one or more of the following dissatisfiers: (1) the confidence factor, (2) the emotional factor, (3) the trust factor, (4) the fit factor, and (5) the listening factor.

The Confidence Factor

Even an organization that is hailed as a "great place to work" by the outside world can suffer slings and arrows from its own employees. Where the outside world sees market share and impressive quarterly results, the employees see only disarray. Amidst this perceived chaos, employees have a difficult time grasping the overall strategy. Even where there is a clear-cut strategy, they often do not see how it is connected to the long-term mission and health of the organization. In such a situation, a loss of confidence and hope can invade the psyche of a key employee, causing him or her to think the grass is greener in another company where there appears to be more focus. Key employees simply do not want to be in an organization that they do not feel is going to win.

The Emotional Factor

Decisions to leave an organization are often based not on facts but on emotion. For example, when key employees leave an organization, they frequently cite lack of recognition, inadequate reward, or too little focus on their personal development as reasons for their departure. It often turns out that the organization is, in fact, recognizing, rewarding, and developing the employee. Emotion, however, has obscured the facts, and image has become more important than reality. Employees in such a mental state interpret the organization's perceived failure to recognize, reward, and develop them as clear signals that they are not valued. In such a situation, they feel that they have no choice but to move on.

The Trust Factor

On their way out the door, key employees often say, "I don't feel that I can trust the organization. There were too many broken promises and commitments that were not kept. They were not loyal to me. Why should I remain loyal to them?" Employees perceive trust as a two-way street: it begins with the employer, and then they respond likewise. A broken promise, whether implicit or explicit, breaks the underpinnings that support this tenuous trust paradigm. Too often, an exiting employee will cite a specific broken promise as one of the chief reasons for leaving. Invariably, when this information is brought back to the employee's manager, the manager will not have any recollection of the incident—further proof that too many managers take their commitments far too lightly.

The Fit Factor

Key employees who dedicate themselves to their organizations need to feel that they fit—that their values, principles, and ethics are in sync with those of the organization. We frequently hear exiting employees say, "I didn't fit in with the team like I used to." It is much easier to leave a team that you don't like—or more importantly, a team that you believe does not like you.

The Listening Factor

Key employees need to believe that leaders, managers, and fellow employees are listening to them. This is perhaps the most frequently cited reason departing employees leave an organization—they believe that they are not being heard. It often turns out that, ironically, the manager is listening to the employee. By the time this fact becomes apparent, however, it is usually too late.

Powerful Conversations are the best way to address these dissatisfiers. While High-Impact Leaders do not schedule Powerful Conversations with their key employees in order to discuss potential dissatisfiers explicitly, they make sure they stay in touch. This constant contact allows them to leap into a Powerful Conversation at the first hint of a dissatisfier. In the process of making a connection, uncovering wants and needs, and making clear commitments, High Impact Leaders can:

- Restore confidence, if that has become a dissatisfier
- Remove misguided emotion, if that has become a dissatisfier
- Rebuild trust, if that has become a dissatisfier
- Reassure fit, if that has become a dissatisfier
- Recommit to listening, if that has become a dissatisfier

In short, a Powerful Conversation is ideally suited to address whatever issue is threatening retention of the key employee.

PROACTIVE RETENTION STRATEGIES

Powerful Conversations, then, are ideally suited for unearthing and driving out dissatisfiers. In this fashion, they operate essentially as a reactive mechanism. But Powerful Conversations can also serve as a proactive mechanism for retention purposes. In particular, Powerful Conversations allow High-Impact Leaders to lay a foundation with a top performer that promotes overall job satisfaction and prevents dissatisfiers from ever developing. I would like to end this chapter by pointing out some specific, proactive strategies High-Impact Leaders employ to ensure that they win the retention wars.

>   *They build confidence and hope through vision and strategy.* High-Impact Leaders spend a lot of time and energy in Powerful Conversations making sure their vision and strategy are connected to the key satisfiers of top performers. They also invite these top performers into the process of creating and defining that vision. They know that the more connected key personnel are to the overall vision and strategy, the more they are likely to feel confident—and the less likely they are to jump ship.

>   *They practice the art of paying attention.* High-Impact Leaders consciously pay attention to their top employees. Merely having Powerful Conversations with them is one form of attention. In addition, during the Powerful Conversation, the High-Impact

Leader makes sure the top performer is feeling rewarded, recognized, and developed, and strives to identify specific wants and needs in those regards. High-Impact Leaders use Powerful Conversations to make top performers feel that they are more important than the business (which, in a sense, they are). And they do all of this in a genuine way—for if it is forced, it will come off as artificial and prove to be counterproductive in the long run. Given the numerous meetings, jammed schedules, and daily crunch, you might wonder whether such attention is necessary. It is. Just ask any leader who has ever lost one of his or her key employees at a key time because of unintentional neglect.

They build commitment, loyalty, and trust. High-Impact Leaders recognize that more trust helps retain more key employees. During Powerful Conversations with top performers, High-Impact Leaders therefore focus on making and meeting commitments. Indeed, as we discussed in Chapter 6, commitment is the foundation of trust. So, High-Impact Leaders make sure they follow through on what they say they are going to do with respect to key employees. They also demonstrate caring so that deeper trust will blossom. When High-Impact Leaders work at building commitment, loyalty, and trust with key employees, they almost always get it back.

They build and maintain relationships. It is a mistake to believe the close one-on-one relationships leaders might enjoy with top performers will, in themselves, keep those employees in place. Dissatisfiers always trump personal relationships. Still, close personal relationships can be a powerful force in retention. In a calculated yet genuine way, High-Impact Leaders use Powerful Conversations to build one-on-one relationships with key people. They know the names and ages of their children and important people in their lives. They control turnover among key employees by making departure from the organization a painful thought, difficult to consider, and very personal.

They create clear communications systems. Finally, High-Impact Leaders use Powerful Conversations to ensure that a key employee is tied into what he or she needs to know. High-Impact Leaders know that when key employees feel uninformed or not listened to, they also feel that the organization doesn't need them (and that they, in turn, don't need the organization).

Today, people can't work much harder or longer, and they have more choices in terms of their employment. The leverage has shifted from the employer to the employee. Those managers and organizations that can keep the lines of communication open will protect their back doors from hungry recruiters. Such a fundamental shift in thinking is required to win today's retention wars.

10

THE VOICE
OF LEADERSHIP

ALL GREAT LEADERS develop and cultivate a distinct voice of leadership. Through tone and message, this voice embodies a leader's values and goals. It also projects his or her drive and personality. A strong voice of leadership is broadcast consistently and clearly in all communication, whether in speeches, memos, e-mails, board meetings, or interactions in the hallway. This voice influences and guides the organization, shaping its values, attitudes, and culture. When a High-Impact Leader has a strong voice of leadership, it reverberates among his or her peers and followers and throughout the organization.

I have visited hundreds of companies in my leadership development work. One of the ways I measure the impact of a leader is by listening for the echoes of his or her voice throughout the organization. In successful organizations—those with strong earnings, growth, market share, and stability—you can hear that echo loud and clear. The voice of leadership emanates from a single High-Impact Leader or a senior team of High-Impact Leaders. It is amplified throughout the organization by Passionate Champions in tune with the message.

We work in an era when organizations spend millions annually on communication strategies, mission statements, and value statements. Most organizations recognize the necessity of broadcasting a strong message up, down, and across the ranks. The answer, however, is not in expensive programs, knowledge management strategies, or corporate intranets. These tools help, to be sure. But too often, organizations neglect the most obvious and least expensive tool. For it is through Powerful Conversations that High-Impact Leaders develop a voice of leadership that resonates throughout the organization.

MASTERING THE LEADERSHIP VOICE

Mark Tolosky is the CEO of Baystate Medical Center and the COO of Baystate Health System, located in Western Massachusetts. He is one of the best examples I know of a High-Impact Leader who consciously and continually works on mastering his voice of leadership.

I first met Mark more than four years ago when I became consultant to his organization's Agenda for Change. In one of our early meetings, I asked Mark to explain how he got his message across to the organization. He answered me quickly and decisively, as if the question was something he thought about daily. The passion behind his words convinced me that he was committed to developing his voice of leadership so that he could translate his message effectively.

"For example, every employee who comes into the system attends an orientation," Mark said. "I make it a point to be at every one I can. The orientation is such an important time and people are really open to my message then. I tell them about the values and principles that I stand for and that our system stands for. I tell them about the importance of our patients, the community, and our overall mission."

I remember asking him how he really got his message across. He told me he liked to use stories. He found it most effective to describe events that had happened in the system that exemplified the organization's values and principles—the important feelings that emerged in encounters with patients, families, and staff, the ways in which people helped each other, and so on.

"What we do is very important," Mark said. "If you don't share what's in your heart, you are cheating your employees because they will be confused about what you really want."

Over the next year, I actively listened for Mark's voice in the words of others. His impact, I observed, was consistently strong across the system in the various hospitals and related businesses. Everyone knew what Mark Tolosky stood for, what he wanted, and what he was committed to. As I got to know Mark better, I learned that he really did consciously work on his voice of leadership. He saw it as ongoing work.

How has this paid off? In the midst of a national and global health care crisis, with so many health care organizations losing money, suffering through massive layoffs, and in many cases functioning in crisis mode,

Baystate Health System continues strong. In as rough a geographic economy and position as one can find, Baystate is maintaining financial balance and keeping its best people. Why? Because the leaders there continue to bring their mission, vision, and operating principles to life through their operations. When an organization spends time building values and openly discussing what's right, what's wrong, and what needs to change, great things happen.

The senior leadership team at Baystate, led by Mark and the president, Michael Daly, meets every month and spends two hours just working on the voice of leadership and the Agenda for Change. Team members talk openly about what's going right and what's going wrong, both within the team and within the organization. They use Powerful Conversations to unearth all facts and assumptions and determine action items.

Between their meetings, team members make commitments to meet with each other to discuss ongoing operations. They dig in deep during these occasions, so that there are no hidden agendas. If they need help, they get it. They don't deny the existence of a problem. They understand that all organizations have problems; the only shameful thing is not facing those problems.

The ultimate purpose of these meetings is to drive strategy. They are not "soft meetings" called to discuss feelings. The leaders on the senior leadership team talk about what they believe and what they need, what they feel about the strategy, how it's working and not working, and how they need to work together in different ways to get the results they are looking for. It's sometimes tough, but they are committed to the process. In fact, one of the senior leaders on the team, Elliott Kellman, is the guardian of the process. The rest of Baystate's senior leaders—powerful business and medical leaders with jammed schedules and a limited amount of time—are full participants in the process, as are Baystate's leaders at the individual affiliates within its system. Collectively, they see the value and importance of this process in meeting their leadership mandate and goals.

The voice of leadership at Baystate is strong. People within the organization at all levels use the same terms to focus on their critical success factors and live up to their operating principles. They get results. Mike Daly and Mark Tolosky have deliberately developed their voice of leadership, used Powerful Conversations together, and created Passionate Champions to push the process down through the organization. That is what High-Impact Leadership is all about.

BROADCASTING THE VOICE OF LEADERSHIP

Think of the strong voices in history that still echo today. Without political office or position of power, without sanction or support, Martin Luther King, Jr., nevertheless projected a powerful message of nonviolent protest, racial integration, and equality. Despite the cacophony of other, hateful voices, King repeated his message over and over. The message proved to be powerful and it resonated. It was picked up by hundreds of people, then thousands, and then millions. It became a force that demanded action and social change. It rings as strongly today—no longer King's dream but ours, even though the source of the voice is tragically no longer with us.

More recently, Ronald Reagan exhorted a nation to feel good about itself and got America working again. His words had that type of effect. Nelson Mandela demanded first freedom and then justice, bringing unity to a nation that seemed irreparably scarred, unable to focus on anything but vengeance. Aung San Suu Kyi, forbidden to speak publicly in Myanmar, nevertheless delivers a resounding message with her simple and persistent call for fair elections.

A voice of leadership can have profound impact on those who hear it. Listen to what historian Doris Kearns Goodwin said in an interview with Linkage's Global Institute for Leadership Development concerning the distinctive voice of Franklin D. Roosevelt:

> Roosevelt had such confidence in himself and in the country, and in the democratic system of government, that somehow he exuded his own confidence into other people. Those who worked with him, like Frances Perkins, his Secretary of Labor, would say that when she left his office she felt somehow buoyed by his trust in her and his confidence that she could do her job. And then she had more confidence in herself. Somehow he was able to project that confidence, which is also a form of trust. Confidence in another person is trust in that person. And then it just becomes a multiplying factor. He projected it onto his Cabinet, they projected it onto their employees, and then in a larger sense, the whole administration projected it onto the country at large.

The challenge is the same in process and technique for those who lead within organizations today. Striving to bring about top performance or realize the power of strategic, organization-wide alignment, a leader speaks the words that crystallize the vision. Defining who we are and where we want to go, a leader's voice forges a coordinated effort and makes the daily action steps happen.

High-Impact Leaders are never embarrassed or hesitant about repeating their messages. To the contrary, they constantly look for new ways to utter the simple words that reflect their mission, vision, and values. The message spreads from the leader to the organization at large, appearing on entranceways, in hallways, on plastic cards, at the top of stationery, in the midst of annual reports, and throughout company-wide e-mails.

The path this message follows is what I previously described as achievability, believability, and transferability. A leader envisions an achievable, though perhaps lofty, goal and expresses that goal as a message. Those thoughts and words appear constantly in the leader's speeches, conversations, voice mails, e-mails, and memos. Slowly—sometimes rapidly—the message is understood. If it is a convincing, sincere, and meaningful message—and if there is trust in the leader—it is embraced. The early recipients of the message are the ones who respond to it most intimately. They become the agents of change, the missionaries of believability. They amplify the message, serving as relay stations to help spread it through their departments and project groups, the places where work actually gets done. High-Impact Leaders know their message has gotten across when it is picked up by others in the organization, becoming part of everyday speech and thought. You never hear people at Microsoft say, "I'm not sure what Bill Gates is committed to." At GE, everyone knows Jack Welch's goal. The transferability of the message in those companies is complete.

When a leader succeeds in transferring his or her message, it provides a framework for thought and a conduit for action. A message projected through a strong voice of leadership can and does affect the way people think, act, work, and behave. It projects their goals and values and becomes part of the way they dream and see, configure and plan.

High-Impact Leaders I have known talk about communication in a reverent way. They have learned—and they are acutely conscious of this fact—that it is their voice that permits them to advance their agenda. Their formula? They create the message, transmit it through a voice, and then repeat it over and over again until it is acid clear.

Consider the following story that further illustrates the effect a strong voice of leadership can have. At a recent leadership development meeting I attended, the president of a prestigious financial institution spoke to other top leaders in his company about the importance of the personal touch in being a real leader. I found it extremely ironic. Here was the high-powered leader of a financial powerhouse stressing the "soft stuff." He told his fellow leaders specific stories of how he had personally reached out to people up, down, and across the organization. He spoke of inviting young people to his home to share dinners with his family. It was a theme he relayed from the heart.

Then the president moved on to address the importance of coaching. His earlier comments seemed to resonate in this light. He spoke of leadership as a privilege and called on the leaders in the room to work humbly and sincerely in providing direction for others. He kept emphasizing the personal touch. To illustrate, he referenced a recent message of encouragement he had received from the firm's chairman. The chairman had been flying in a plane in the middle of the night and had suddenly decided to leave a voice mail message for the president, merely because the chairman had thought of him. At the leadership development meeting, the president told the other leaders of the firm that he had found special meaning in the simplicity and caring of the chairman's message—that it had somehow been more lasting and profound for that reason.

The president said that he, too, would like to be remembered for his notes, e-mails, and voice mails—his efforts at connecting in personal ways. I was struck by how many people in his audience made note of this. Everyone seemingly understood, in his or her own way, how this value and belief could manifest itself in their work. It was a quiet message, but it seemed to sink in strongly. The president's voice had projection. I was certain this was not the first time his voice had resonated through the company's worldwide offices.

As I got to know the people in the firm better, I checked for the president's voice of leadership. Was it there? Was it consistent? Had it sunk in widely? Did people internalize his message? I interviewed 20 of the company's leaders from around the world, geographically dispersed in places like Hong Kong, Singapore, London, and New York. And I heard the president's voice loud and clear in offices, conference calls, and shared taxi rides. Stories spilled out of the commitments the president had made and the values he had professed. His way of connecting with each leader was consistent in content—yet the connection was always individual and personal.

DEVELOPING THE VOICE OF LEADERSHIP
In a sense, the voice of leadership is a long, unbroken Powerful Conversation with individuals and the organization at large. The conversation goes on, consistent in message and gaining power through its clarity and repetition.

Like a Powerful Conversation, the voice of leadership also achieves its strength through the sincerity of its connection. It fosters learning and strengthens relationships. It builds the trust that is a binding force for the organization. It promotes loyalty and commitment.

High-Impact Leaders acknowledge that the voice of leadership develops slowly over time. It emerges through trial and error—by grinding it out in the trenches and frequently stumbling in the mud. It grows and gains in legitimacy from active connections of Say and Do. In my experience, though, too many leaders fail to articulate a voice of leadership because they project a message that is inconsistent with their actions. Message and actions must match seamlessly to foster the desired result—a strong voice of leadership.

Perception is a must. The message is always subject to translation by the listener. It gets filtered through beliefs and values that may or may not be shared. Some leaders understandably experience great frustration if their message is not received properly. They often fail to understand that they can control, to a significant extent, how that message is received. They can do so by proper use of medium. The voice of leadership consists of both message and medium—and too often the latter is neglected in favor of the former. Clear communication is forever at the whim of interpretations of tone, body language, and context. Timing is important; messages are received better in some contexts than others. And, of course, trust helps the message become much clearer.

The more experience leaders gain, the more aware they are of the way people respond to their message. As leaders grow into responsibility and rise in rank, they also become more economical in their use of language. They refine their message into fewer and fewer words in an attempt to capture core meaning as well as core values. There is beauty in simplicity. A simple message seems to take root more readily. Like a parable, a simple message lasts longer and is passed on more easily.

This is why great leaders often use stories to translate their messages. Stories connect and become part of the lore of the organization. A story can translate a leader's voice, especially when that story is repeated and contemplated throughout the organization. It can reflect values and principles without overburdening the listener with theory. What leaders say in the stories they tell eventually finds its way into stories others tell about them.

GUIDING AND ENABLING WITH THE VOICE OF LEADERSHIP

The voice of leadership ripples outward in the smallest ways, creating unimaginable collective impact. Consider the number of "voice touches" a leader has with those around him or her in the course of the day. There are casual conversations, letters, e-mails, speeches, and scores of meetings. I make it a point every day to create specific opportunities to use my voice to touch those around me. Each day within Linkage—even days chock-full of meetings—I try to send at least two e-mails and make two phone calls to employees within our organization. This allows me to reach four important people inside of Linkage every day, over and above those I work with on a regular basis. Doing so provides me the opportunity to clarify my own voice of leadership and drive home my own message.

A human resources officer with a subsidiary of Monsanto recently reinforced my belief in the importance of daily touches. She mentioned that one day, struck by an idea around an initiative she had begun, she sent along an e-mail to the president of Monsanto. Within hours, he responded with a very clear message. He indicated that he had heard what she said, mentioned specifically his own thoughts and feelings, and made a small commitment to her regarding the program. It was a minute gesture, but totally in character with that leader's voice of leadership. My friend at Monsanto was deeply moved. "I'd go to the wall for this guy. Just because he heard me," she said. The power of this kind of connection is enormous.

The voice of leadership is used in deliberate, developmental work as well, which is why it is so critical in coaching. Leaders who have a seasoned, clear voice of leadership are the best coaches. They spend a significant amount of time using their voice of leadership to guide others toward the right actions and the right decisions, providing feedback, pathways, and perspective. They guide in accordance with one vigilant, sacrosanct principle: constancy. Being consistent is the secret to ensuring that a leader's voice of leadership is heard in every coaching session in the same way. Most importantly, High-Impact Leaders use the voice of leadership to provide confidence. They enable others around them to win by expressing hope and optimism in such a way—through the voice of leadership—that others believe in their own power and ability.

BREAKDOWNS IN THE VOICE OF LEADERSHIP
Breakdowns in the voice of leadership result in diminished impact. When a leader feels that his or her impact has weakened, it is important to assess whether he or she is having any problems in transmitting messages or articulating his or her voice.

Some leaders believe that rapid shifts in their messages or the tone of their messages constitute an effective motivator. They think that outbursts or unpredictable decisions—in other words, a shifting voice of leadership—keep people on their toes and make them work harder to understand the content and meaning of a leader's messages. Such an approach is misguided: it may have some value in the short term but is destructive in the long view. The organizations that display the highest levels of performance for the longest periods of time thrive on consistency, clarity, and openness, not capriciousness and fear.

At other times, a voice of leadership can weaken because the leader's own enthusiasm weakens. At a lonely moment, some leaders find themselves asking, "Is what I'm doing really significant? Is what I'm saying truly important?" Sometimes this is due to a temporary lapse in courage. We are all surrounded by naysayers. It seems to be part of human nature to want to sap the energy from someone who exhibits confidence, optimism, and vision. Reconnecting to inner principles can provide a renewed confidence—and a reinvigorated voice of leadership.

A leader, though reflective and self-examining, recognizes the necessity of always moving forward. Rick Pitino, coach of the Boston Celtics, describes such a concept as being 98/2—that is, leaders should be optimistic and hopeful 98 percent of the time and should try to be so during the other 2 percent of the time. All of us have our 2 percent moments; these can be especially burdensome for a leader. I keep the phrase *98/2* in mind every day. I know I've got to keep moving.

REFOCUSING THE VOICE OF LEADERSHIP

For all High-Impact Leaders, it occasionally becomes necessary to refocus the voice of leadership, particularly when it has weakened for some reason.

It is most important at these times to assess the facts and assumptions that underlie the diminished impact in leadership voice. Under such circumstances, leaders must try to define clearly the circumstances in which the leadership voice has weakened or varied. Asking hard questions helps. High-Impact Leaders do not let themselves off the hook. They know the real facts are the ones that provide solutions. They ask questions like: Am I losing some of my Passionate Champions? Am I letting people down? Am I being unclear again as to what I want and need? Have I not delivered the goods? Am I expecting too much of others and forcing them into commitments that they can't meet? Have I broken commitments and promises?

With the proper mind-set, High-Impact Leaders can repair a great deal of the damage that emerges through such questioning. If they need to reconnect with their Passionate Champions, they can do so. If they have let others down by breaking commitments, they can acknowledge it openly and move on to rebuild the lost trust. In such circumstances it is important to consult a close ally—someone trusted to relay honest criticism in testing out ideas and new approaches.

Most of the leadership voice breakdowns I have personally experienced revolve around clarity. I swallow my pride, acknowledge that I am still not all the way there, and redouble my personal commitment to make sure my messages are heard in the clearest ways. I will then spend more time in getting more specific, concrete, and detailed in my e-mails and messages, even distributing voice mails to those around me to make sure I am saying the right thing in the right way, focusing not only on my needs but also on the needs of others.

This may sound like it requires a lot of energy. It does. But it is part and parcel of growth as a leader. When my voice of leadership breaks down, I don't fault others for the resulting loss of impact. I know it is my responsibility as a leader to make sure my message is heard. Knowing that most leaders are blessed or cursed with an overabundance of pride makes it somewhat easier to let go of some of my own pride and work to refocus my own voice of leadership.

CREATING THE REAL YOU
The voice of leadership projects outward, but the conversation also must take place within. It is frequently said that a leader leads with the heart, and I believe this to be true. Throughout this book, we have stressed the importance of authenticity in generating Powerful Conversations. Expressions of heartfelt feelings, sincerity, vulnerability, and truth make the strong connections that enable the sharing of real wants and needs.

But the work of the leader begins with the self. The honest unveiling of wants and needs must start within a leader's own heart. It is from this source that a leader really learns how to exert power. Great leaders gain their impact when they are authentic with others. Doing so requires that they first be authentic with themselves.

The High-Impact Leaders I have observed are in a continual process of learning and development. This learning is focused in two directions. It is aimed outward, on the bigger issues involved in running an organization and competing in the global marketplace. But it is also aimed inward, at an exploration of meandering paths in the landscape of the leaders' own spirits.

It is not just about exploring weakness and pain. The authenticity I am speaking of is more focused on revealing truth. Real learning is about confronting truth. Yet so often, in our dialogues with our own selves, we duck the truth and fail to unveil our most precious and treasured wants and needs, even to ourselves.

I want to end this book with an exploration of how you can learn to be honest within yourself. I want to describe how, in a journey toward great leadership, you can use Powerful Conversations to create the real you.

I find this inward-focused dialogue to be among the most difficult of conversations. My upbringing contributes to this challenge—one part *Angela's Ashes* and the other part *Good Will Hunting.* Growing up an Irish Catholic in Boston, I am used to the gesture of confession and I well understand its importance and ritual meaning. Yet, I am also equally skilled at dodging its embarrassment and painful honesty.

As teenagers, my friends and I would go to the Italian church for confession because we knew that the priest there spoke little English. If we whispered our confession quickly enough, he would be unable to understand most of what we had said and we would wind up with only a small penance. We had gotten away with something—dodged the truth and its repercussions—if we were assigned only a few Our Fathers. I remember the nearly irrepressible laughter when one of us returned from the confessional one day to say 10 Our Fathers. We knew by the number of Our Fathers that he had done something particularly rotten and we could only imagine what that might be. But more than that, we laughed because we knew he had gotten caught.

I think many of us are like that—unwilling and uneager to dig at the truth of what is going on inside. When we avoid the truth, we think we are getting away with something, but we are really robbing ourselves of power. Not wanting to deal with real things, we put them aside and don't think about them. We create hidden dialogue inside ourselves. This clouds our knowledge of ourselves and muffles the way we project our character into the real world. It mutes our message and creates gaps between Say and Do, between the values and truths we espouse and the ones we actually use.

All of this can be especially demanding for leaders who exert a tremendous amount of energy in trying to lead. Organizations take whatever we can give. They are like suckling children that need to nurse, even if this is occasionally beyond the mother's ability to produce milk. It is necessary for a leader to replenish his or her spirit, confidence, and sense of will and vision. Without doing so, each projection of power leaves us drained of energy and less connected with the meaning of our most important efforts.

There are ways we can advance our dialogue with ourselves in order to replenish and strengthen our voice of leadership. It starts first with understanding the importance of connecting inwardly. We probe in a committed way to uncover real wants and needs and all of the interrelated facts and assumptions. We determine what those are and look honestly at what it will take to reach our own satisfiers. We debate our choices and determine what is possible. The path becomes clearer. We can begin, if we are honest and work hard at it, to make commitments to ourselves that lead to achieving the results our own spirits demand.

Self-understanding takes time, and it is a long, slow, demanding process. There are threats and risks, and we long to escape from truth and avoid any penance, even if the confession will free us to move forward. Such a process is essential for strengthening our personal and professional relationships and makes us into High-Impact Leaders. It helps to have tools. I hope this book provides some support in that direction.

Remember three words to guide you in the conversations still to come: candor, clarity, and commitment. Despite the risk, lead with your vulnerability and put your fears in front of you. Each day will bring opportunities to advance new agendas and lead from strength.

A POWERFUL CONVERSATIONS TOOLBOX

INTRODUCTION

Mastering the discipline of Powerful Conversations requires practice. To that end, this appendix contains a number of tools relating to Powerful Conversations. High-Impact Leaders use these tools to shape their conversations and ensure that they are, in fact, Powerful Conversations, i.e., that they advance agendas, promote learning, and strengthen relationships.

Specifically, this appendix contains the following tools:

Tool 1: Planning, Conducting, and Measuring Powerful Conversations

Tool 2: The Tower of Power

Tool 3: The Leadership Assessment Instrument (LAI)

Tool 4: The Trust Tool

Tool 5: The Change Tool

Tool 6: The Retention Tool

Most of these tools are referenced or explained in the text of the book. For your convenience, cross-references to the text are included. You should view each tool in conjunction with the referenced text for complete understanding.

All of the tools contained in this appendix are property of Linkage, Inc. ("Linkage") and are reprinted here with Linkage's permission. If you are interested in reproducing, distributing, or using any of these tools for purposes other than your own self-development, you must obtain Linkage's prior permission. You can do so by contacting Linkage at (781) 862-3157.

TOOL 1: PLANNING, CONDUCTING, AND MEASURING POWERFUL CONVERSATIONS

In Chapter 2, we detailed the structure and impact of Powerful Conversations. The guidelines contained in the following tool will further help you plan, conduct, and measure your own Powerful Conversations (as well as observe those of others).

Planning Powerful Conversations

Step One: Organize the conversation around your own agenda—and anticipate the agendas of others.

Step Two: Define your desired outcome—and anticipate the desired outcomes of others.

Step Three: Identify natural points of intersection between your agenda/desired outcome and the agendas/desired outcomes of others.

Step Four: Think of any other factors or issues that might potentially get you off track—and decide how you might defuse them.

Step Five: Pay attention to timing—make sure you don't try to have the Powerful Conversation at the wrong time, which will ruin your best-laid plans.

Conducting Powerful Conversations

Stage One: Introduction
- Set up your own agenda with an honest feeling, belief, or idea.
- Hint: don't be afraid to express vulnerability (as long as it's genuine).
- Critical success factor: *candor.*

Stage Two: Middle
- Discuss the issue, probing for the wants/needs of the other person and then clearly stating your own wants/needs.
- Hint: always start with the other person's agenda, and then move toward your agenda (pull others in, don't push).
- Critical success factor: *clarity.*

Stage Three: Closing
- Nail down the next steps and make sure you (and the other person) got what was wanted out of the conversation.
- Hint: be explicit with respect to "to do's."
- Critical success factor: *commitment.*

Measuring Powerful Conversations

There are three outcomes of a Powerful Conversation:

1. Advanced agendas
2. Shared learning
3. Stronger relationship

You can track the impact of your Powerful Conversation by using these measurements and a matrix similar to the one in Figure A-1.

Alternatively, you can determine whether there has been a two-way Powerful Conversation by employing a series of simple questions such as:

Advanced agendas
- Ask yourself: did I get what I needed?
- Ask the other person: did you get what you needed?

Shared learning
- Ask yourself: did I learn something?
- Ask the other person: did you learn something?

Stronger relationship
- Ask yourself: do I feel our relationship is stronger?
- Ask the other person: do you feel our relationship is stronger?

Naturally, you should state these questions in your own language and in your own communication style. However you ask them, make sure you get the information that reveals whether a Powerful Conversation has taken place.

FIGURE A-1

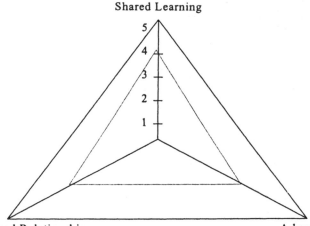

Shared Learning

Strengthened Relationship   Advanced Agenda

TOOL 2: THE TOWER OF POWER

In Chapter 2, we discussed at length how you can use the Tower of Power (see Figure A-2) to structure your Powerful Conversations. The pages that follow set forth the Tower and provide some potential uses, rules of progression, and helpful hints.

FIGURE A-2

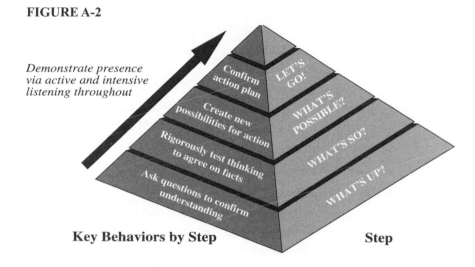

Key Behaviors by Step   Step

The "Swamp"

Potential Uses of the Tower of Power

There are four primary ways you can use the Tower of Power in regard to Powerful Conversations:

1.   To prepare for your Powerful Conversations
2.   To conduct your Powerful Conversations
3.   As a tool in coaching interactions
4.   As a diagnostic instrument to observe the conversations of others

Rules of Progression for the Tower of Power

Step One: "What's Up?"
- Start by asking "What's going on?", "What's wrong?", or "What's up?"
- Get agreement on the issue and the basic contours of that issue.

Step Two: "What's So?"
- Spend time unearthing the key facts, as well as the underlying assumptions driving those facts.
- Get agreement on facts and assumptions before moving to Step Three.

Step Three: "What's Possible?"
- Review at least two to four opportunities/options/possibilities for action.
- Confirm whether the option you choose "takes us where we need to go" (if it does not, return to Step Two to get back on track).
- Get agreement on options before moving to Step Four.

Step Four: "Let's Go!"
- Identify and discuss action steps.
- Say specifically, "Did you get what you needed? Are you okay with what we decided? How do you feel about the process and the outcome?"
- Confirm—and reconfirm—commitments made.

Helpful Hints for Using the Tower of Power

- Keep in mind that the Tower is particularly valuable with respect to difficult conversations (see Chapter 5)—it can help you prepare for those conversations, as well as guide you through them.
- Never skip a step in the Tower (e.g., don't go from Step One to Step Three, or from Step Two to Step Four).
- Make sure you have the necessary agreement before you proceed to the next step.
- Return to a step if necessary (e.g., in Step Three, if it is clear that some assumptions are not yet on the table, return to Step Two).
- Be on the alert for "hidden dialogue" (i.e., inner beliefs or opinions that remain unstated) that might obviate the agreements that you have reached—and seek to uncover that hidden dialogue so that you can get real agreement.
- Reiterate the commitments in Step Four—and make them explicit.
- Listen throughout.

TOOL 3: THE LEADERSHIP ASSESSMENT INSTRUMENT (LAI)

In Chapter 3, we introduced the Leadership Assessment Instrument (LAI) in conjunction with our analysis of the different types of Powerful Conversations. The LAI is a 360° instrument based upon the Global Institute Leadership Model (see Figure A-3), a researched model developed by Linkage, Inc. in conjunction with Warren Bennis that captures the elements of high-performance leadership. The pages that follow set forth that model and provide definitions of the leadership knowledge areas, skills, and competencies that are contained in that model, as well as definitions of the two components that make up each leadership competency in the model. We also provide a self-scoring sample of the competency items contained on the LAI that will give you a snapshot of your own leadership strengths and weaknesses. Please note, however, that you can obtain a full picture of your leadership capabilities through the LAI only by taking the entire instrument (which consists of 75 items in total and tests for both leadership competencies and leadership skills).

FIGURE A-3

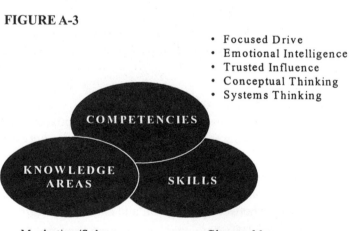

- Focused Drive
- Emotional Intelligence
- Trusted Influence
- Conceptual Thinking
- Systems Thinking

COMPETENCIES

KNOWLEDGE AREAS

SKILLS

- Marketing/Sales
- Running the Business
- Finance
- Human Capital
- Strategic Planning

- Change Management
- Coaching/Mentoring
- Communication
- Negotiation
- Problem Solving

The Leadership Knowledge Areas—Definitions

- *Marketing/Sales:* The knowledge required to market and sell your organization's products, services, and programs

- *Running the Business:* The knowledge required to coordinate the efforts and subparts of your organization (operationally and otherwise)
- *Finance:* The knowledge required to interpret financial and economic trends (and take appropriate action in response)
- *Human Capital:* The knowledge required to employ, deploy, and maximize the talents of the people within your organization.
- *Strategic Planning:* The knowledge required to set long-term and short-term yardsticks for your organization

The Leadership Skills—Definitions

- *Change Management:* The skill of adapting to and thriving in times of internal and external change
- *Coaching/Mentoring:* The skill of mastering a comfortable coaching style and using it strategically to improve performance
- *Communication:* The skill of communicating with and relating to a broad range of people internally and externally
- *Negotiation:* The skill of arriving at and reaching understandings and agreements with a broad range of people, internally and externally
- *Problem Solving:* The skill of employing analytical abilities, pragmatism, and other tools to resolve complex problems in a variety of contexts

The Leadership Competencies—Definitions

- *Focused Drive:* The competency of focusing on a goal and harnessing your energy in order to meet that goal—a balance between *focus* and *drive*
- *Emotional Intelligence:* The competency of understanding and mastering your emotions (and those of others) in a way that instills confidence—a balance between *perception* and *emotional maturity*
- *Trusted Influence:* The competency of evoking trust from others and placing trust in others to enable them to succeed—a balance between *commitment* and *empowerment*
- *Conceptual Thinking:* The competency of conceiving and selecting innovative strategies and ideas for your organization—a balance between *innovation* and *big picture thinking*
- *Systems Thinking:* The competency of connecting processes, events, and structures—a balance between *process orientation* and *mental discipline*

Components of Leadership Competencies

Each of the five leadership competencies is composed of two components, as shown in Figure A-4.

Focused Drive =
- *Focus:* The ability to identify an important goal or vision and to channel efforts at specific targets that support that goal/vision
- *Drive:* The ability to persevere, sacrifice (when necessary), and expend high degrees of energy to reach high levels of performance

Emotional Intelligence =
- *Perception:* The ability to read the emotions and thoughts of others through the use of insight and analytical skills
- *Emotional maturity:* The ability to master emotions and cope with stress in a way that instills confidence, motivates, and enhances group effectiveness

FIGURE A-4

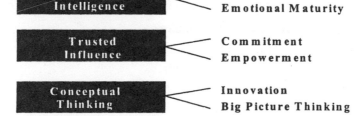
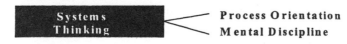

Trusted Influence =
- *Commitment:* The ability to evoke trust from others by keeping commitments, adhering to high ethical standards and principles, and building shared goals/values
- *Empowerment:* The ability to help others reach higher levels of performance through trust, delegation, participation, and coaching

Conceptual Thinking =
- *Innovation:* The ability to create/enhance ideas, products, and services that lead to bottom-line success
- *Big picture thinking:* The ability to see all of the forces, events, entities, and people involved in the situation at hand

Systems Thinking =
- *Process orientation:* The ability to increase overall learning and performance by designing, implementing, and/or connecting processes
- *Mental discipline:* The ability to sort through ambiguity and alternatives in a way that crystallizes and puts ideas into action

Self-Scoring Sample of the LAI

Overview.   To give you an idea of the essence of the LAI—as well as a glimpse of your own potential leadership strengths and weaknesses—we have provided a sample of the 75 items on the LAI. The sample includes 20 items, all of which are related to and representative of the five leadership competencies contained in the model set forth earlier in this tool.

Directions.   Think of your day-to-day work as a leader. In light of this, respond to each of the questions below according to the following scale:

- 1 = I rarely demonstrate this behavior
- 2 = I sometimes demonstrate this behavior
- 3 = I often demonstrate this behavior
- 4 = I very often demonstrate this behavior
- 5 = I always demonstrate this behavior

For each item, place in the blank provided the number that corresponds to how often you believe you demonstrate the behavior captured by the item.

A. FOCUSED DRIVE

Scale Score (1, 2, 3, 4, or 5)

1. I strive to set and achieve ambitious goals rather than settling for the safety of achievable results.   _____
2. I display single-mindedness in directing my energy at key targets.   _____
3. I maintain focus when disruptions might detract attention from key issues and objectives.   _____

4.   I overcome potential stumbling blocks to achieve an objective.   _____

TOTAL FOR FOCUSED DRIVE
(Add scores for #1–4)   _____

B. EMOTIONAL INTELLIGENCE

Scale Score
(1, 2, 3, 4, or 5)

5.   I consider the impact of my own behavior or decisions on other people.   _____

6.   I create a positive environment through the use of sincerity and optimism.   _____

7.   I model how to handle failure by accepting setbacks with grace and renewed determination.   _____

8.   I treat each person differently according to his or her own unique makeup.   _____

TOTAL FOR EMOTIONAL INTELLIGENCE
(Add scores for #5–8)   _____

C. TRUSTED INFLUENCE

Scale Score
(1, 2, 3, 4, or 5)

9.   I create a view of the future that motivates others.

10.   I display a strong commitment to the success of others by providing clear feedback on issues or behavior.   _____

11.   I provide whatever is needed to help others take charge of their work and successfully produce results.   _____

12.   I set a clear example for others by following through on important commitments.   _____

TOTAL FOR TRUSTED INFLUENCE
(Add scores for #9–12)   _____

D. CONCEPTUAL THINKING

Scale Score
(1, 2, 3, 4, or 5)

13.   I ask "What if?" questions to test assumptions and challenge the status quo.   _____

14.   I seek better solutions to problems instead of falling back on obvious answers.   _____

15.   I make connections between and among information, events, etc. that reveal key issues or opportunities.   _____

16. I search for and conceptualize the underlying or systemic causes that drive a problem. _____

TOTAL FOR CONCEPTUAL THINKING (Add scores for #13–16) _____

E. SYSTEMS THINKING

Scale Score (1, 2, 3, 4, or 5)

17. I crystallize thoughts by deliberately and systemically steering through ambiguity and information clutter. _____

18. I adhere to processes to make sure that the right people are involved in a project. _____

19. I take steps to make sure new ideas are integrated with established procedures or processes. _____

20. I thoughtfully reach decisions by reviewing ideas and assumptions with key individuals within the organization. _____

TOTAL FOR SYSTEMS THINKING (add scores for #17–20) _____

Analysis. Now examine your total scores for each of the five leadership competencies (Focused Drive, Emotional Intelligence, Trusted Influence, Conceptual Thinking, and Systems Thinking).

• Which competency has the highest total? _____
   This likely constitutes one of your strongest leadership capabilities.

• Which competency has the lowest total? _____
   This likely comprises a developmental need as you continue to build your leadership capabilities.

   Now, refer back to Chapter 3, where we link the leadership competencies with certain types of Powerful Conversations—for example, Focused Drive is required for Powerful Conversations that actualize strategy, Emotional Intelligence is required for Powerful Conversations that stabilize, and so on. The snapshot this sample offers of a potential strength and weakness among the leadership competencies suggests corresponding types of Powerful Conversations that may constitute strengths and weaknesses, respectively. How does your profile match up?

TOOL 4: THE TRUST TOOL

In Chapter 6, we addressed the subject of Powerful Conversations and trust. This tool will help you continue to work through this critical issue. In particular, it contains three parts: (1) a model indicating the drivers of trust, as captured in the Say-Do relationship (see Figure A-5); (2) a model indicating the dimensions of trust, as captured by the Four C's (see Figure A-6); and (3) a model indicating the levels of trust (see Figure A-7). All three of these models are explained in more depth elsewhere in the book. Taken together, they provide a new way of looking at trust and its relationship to leadership.

The Drivers of Trust: The Say-Do Relationship

FIGURE A-5

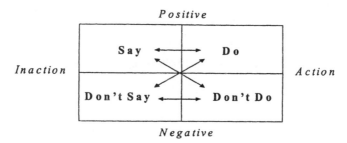

- The horizontal lines in the diagram in Figure A-5 represent how leaders can build and maintain trust—by doing what they say they will do and by not doing things they didn't announce.
- The diagonals, on the other hand, represent where leaders can run into trouble in terms of trust—when they don't do something they said they would do, or when they do something they didn't announce.

The Dimensions of Trust: The Four C's

FIGURE A-6

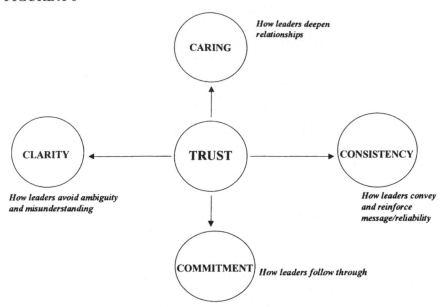

The Levels of Trust

FIGURE A-7

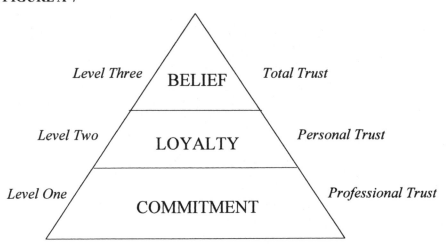

In what level does your relationship with another person (or your organization in general) reside? Use the indicia given here to find out.

Level One: begins with commitment

We consistently . . .
- Listen to real requests
- Clarify—ask specific questions
- Verify exact deliverables
- Check in on expectations

We don't ever . . .
- "Sort of" agree
- Assume the message
- Take requests lightly
- Ignore commitments

Level Two: focuses on relationship

We consistently . . .
- Demonstrate caring
- Give credit
- Warn/advise

- Defend/uphold
- Spend time

We don't ever . . .
- Have damaging emotional outbursts
- Save self at the expense of another
- Take on another in public or behind his or her back
- Pass on a rumor

Level Three: targets principles/values

With conviction, we . . .
- State/share beliefs
- Live shared principles
- Learn/accept others
- Admit mistakes

We don't ever . . .
- Lie (even fib)
- Plagiarize
- Talk north/go south
- Compromise on principles

TOOL 5: THE CHANGE TOOL

In Chapter 7, we discussed how to design and implement an Agenda for Change. If you are interested in defining and mapping your own Agenda for Change, we recommend you consult Chapter 7 for the specific steps and challenges involved. The tool that follows, which we call *Blueprinting* (see Figure A-8), will help in this regard. Specifically, Blueprinting is a front-end tool for identifying and clarifying change initiatives (and the steps required to get there).

FIGURE A-8

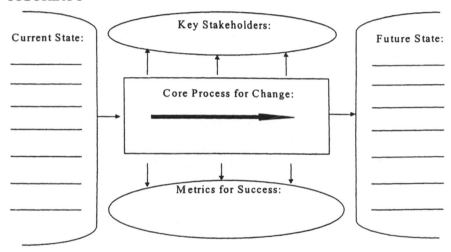

Using the Blueprint

Step One: Define future state
- Look into the future (two to three years, perhaps).
- Write the newspaper headlines you would like to see at that time concerning your organization (however bold or audacious).
- Commit to the future state.

Step Two: Assess current state
- Evaluate the present state of your organization.
- Identify the key aspects and characteristics of the current state of your organization.
- Agree on the current state.

Step Three: Conduct gap analysis
- Compare the current state against your desired future state.
- How large is the gap? What will you need to do to close it? (See Steps Four through Six.)

Step Four: Develop core process for change
- Decide upon specific initiative(s) that will effect the change from current to future state.
- Identify conversations, practices, and day-to-day operations necessary to carry out the initiative(s).
- Set the process (in form of action steps and timetable) for the change initiative(s).

Step Five: Identify key stakeholders
- Determine who will make or break the change process, as well as who has the most to gain or lose from the change.
- Discuss how you will tie those individuals to the change initiative(s).

Step Six: Determine metrics for success
- Identify specific metrics you will use to measure the progress and success of your change initiative(s).
- Consider a full range of metrics (employee feedback, customer feedback, financial results, tangible outputs, etc.) and select the appropriate one depending on the specifics of your change initiative(s).

TOOL 6: THE RETENTION TOOL

In Chapter 9, we examined how leaders can use Powerful Conversations to retain key performers. The tool that follows takes a broader approach (see Figure A-9), setting forth an entire process to improve retention of key people—with Powerful Conversations remaining at the very heart of the process.

FIGURE A-9

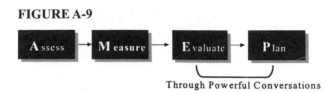

Through Powerful Conversations

Step 1: Assess
- Rank your employees in terms of value to the organization.
- Make sure you rank according to clear and consistent criteria (e.g., productivity, output, competencies, teamwork).
- Use rankings to identify the top third of your employees (this is the group that should be the focus of your retention efforts).

Step 2: Measure
- Measure the replacement costs of the top third so that the organization has a yardstick of market worth.
- Take into consideration all the hard costs associated with replacement, including customer impact, productivity, knowledge, and so on.
- Generate a risk report that captures these replacement costs.

Step 3: Evaluate
- Develop a Powerful Conversation strategy, where you (and/or fellow leaders, as well) have a series of Powerful Conversations with top third to determine their wants, needs, and expectations.
- Focus on satisfiers and dissatisfiers during those Powerful Conversations. (See Chapter 9 for further detail.)
- Generate a vulnerability report that captures key satisfiers that are not being met and dissatisfiers that may exist among your top third.

Step 4: Plan
- Have follow-up Powerful Conversations with your top third to make sure that all wants, needs, expectations, satisfiers, and dissatisfiers are being adequately addressed.

Index